Song Of My Soul:

Hope, Inspiration and Wisdom From A Cancer Survivor

Also by Sheila Ulrich

Wake Up and Live The Life You Love! A Search for Purpose.

Song of My Soul: My Journey To Wellness

Truly Alive
Sheila Ulrich
www.sheilaulrich.com
sheila@sheilaulrich.com

ISBN: 978-1-59916-405-2

Song Of My Soul:

Hope, Inspiration and Wisdom From A Cancer Survivor

Sheila Ulrich

Dedication:

To my three angels,
Carlie, Claire and Connor
Who gave me the courage to continue the journey!

Contents

Chapter 1

The Wake-Up Call

It was just a quiet Monday afternoon in January, but it was special to me. Only six months had passed since I had quit my job and left behind a life-long career. Now I was embarking on something else new.

Tim and I had rearranged our priorities, and family was now at the top of the list. Our lives had spiraled out of control when career, civic and social events tied for first place among our priorities. But we had decided that twelve-year-old Carlie, six-year-old Claire and three-year-old Connor deserved to have a stable and loving home life and Tim and I wanted a less chaotic life too. Carlie, who was in sixth grade that year, had just come home from school, and I was there for her. This was still a new experience for us, one that filled me with gratitude. In all my years of working long hours, I had never understood how much it meant to her to have me there when she came home at the end of the day.

So here I was, providing a warm home on a snowy day. I was happy to be doing it. Also, I was excited about setting up my first home computer. I loved being home, but I still believed my best contributions to my family and the world came through "doing." So I was going to "do something." I would work from home, and this new computer was a big part of that plan.

I barely noticed the ringing, lost as I was among cables, instructions and computer parts, but Carlie brought me the phone. It was my doctor, calling about last week's biopsy.

I'd forgotten there was a biopsy. I'd been through one six months earlier that was no big deal. A spot was removed, biopsy results were normal, and I didn't give it another thought. This time, though, the doctor called to say the results were positive.

Still deciphering computer instructions, I barely heard her. "Positive for what?" I still didn't get it.

She was stuttering and couldn't say the words. "Just tell me, what are you trying to say?" I persisted.

"You have cancer."

I screamed before I realized I was screaming! The terror and horror arose that fast and I fell to the floor. Then it was as if the world stopped and all was silent. In that moment, I was alone and afraid, as if no one else existed.

Where was Tim? I couldn't think or move. Some how I located the telephone number to the hunt club he was hunting at and was able to reach him. All I could say was, "Come home!" Next came a rush of activity. Within hours, I was at a clinic for tests and scheduled for surgery early the next morning. I could barely talk or think, and I cried for hours. Tim finally gave me a sedative to sleep. I had to be on the road at 5:00 am for surgery. Poor Carlie! Looking back now on all that pain and trauma, my heart breaks for her. After just six months, she, Claire and Connor were knocked back down on the list of priorities while Tim and I rushed to make life-and-death decisions. If only I could have really been there for Carlie, talked to her and consoled her as she dealt with her shock, pain and loss. It may have helped her avoid years of suffering and struggling. The wisdom of tomorrow would be such a gift for today, but we only have this moment to live the best we can.

Claire Connor and Carlie -- Sheila and Tim -- Before Cancer

The tumor was on my lower left leg. The first biopsy six months prior had come from a small red spot just above the Achilles tendon of the same leg. Over a period of a year or two, it had grown slightly, so I had it removed. It didn't resemble anything of danger in color, size or shape. The spot was removed on June 1, 1994, the last day of my old career.

That first biopsy was normal, so I forgot about it and got busy adjusting to my new life. For the first time, I spent all summer at home with my kids. We played and swam and visited family and friends.

Two months later, I developed a purplish blister-like spot in the same location. This raised my suspicions. In a routine doctor's visit with my daughter, I asked his opinion about the growth. He said it looked like a ketosis. I was very uncomfortable with that answer, and I vowed to see a specialist.

Still, months went by before I made it a priority. Perhaps I was too afraid to. And I was still a rookie at making my priorities match my values. So it was four months before I had that ominous spot removed.

Again, my dermatologist wasn't concerned. Connor observed the whole procedure. Standing on a little stool at the end of the table, he watched as Dr. Kay removed the spot. We had no premonition of the darkness of that moment or of the days to follow.

Now, I was facing a diagnosis of malignant melanoma and had to have surgery immediately. The doctors were unsure of the extent of the disease, but their uncertainty and extreme concern sent fear through our entire beings. We knew it was very serious. At 5 o'clock the next morning we drove to the hospital for surgery. In a zombie-like state, I went through the motions, not knowing the doctors or the procedures I was to encounter.

During the first procedure, a technician injected dye into multiple spots on my leg to map the drainage of my lymphatic system in the region of the tumor. It was very painful! Still, the emotional trauma far overshadowed the physical pain. For hours I lay alone, crying on the table. The surgeon came to introduce himself. With compassion, he stroked my hair to calm me, and I knew I liked this man. He felt my pain, and it touched my heart to know he cared.

Dr. James was his name. It's a name I will remember for the rest of my life. He was a plastic surgeon. Because of the location of the tumor, I needed a skin graft to replace the tissue that would be removed from my lower left leg.

Dr. James explained I would have a wide local excision that would remove tissue two inches around the tumor. The location of the tumor prevented him from pulling surrounding skin to close the incision. Instead, they outlined the same amount of skin on my buttocks, which would replace the skin on my leg. I would have to keep my lower leg immobile until the graft began to grow onto the new site.

I had never had surgery or general anesthesia. Tim was by my side, giving me strength to take the next step. No words could comfort either of us. There were no words, only tears. All the nurses and doctors were kind and loving, trying to comfort us. The anesthesiologist explained the procedures he would use, and then I drifted off.

Nearly five hours later, I awoke shaking and frozen. I was covered in layers of hot blankets in an attempt to warm my trembling body. I heard voices as if from a distance, and I tried to return to reality. I saw Tim and thought, "This is real!" I had retreated to a place of comfort and safety, where the earthly world didn't exist and I was an observer of it all.

The pain enveloped my whole body. Since I couldn't be moved for a few days, and my leg had to remain immobile, Dr. James had specifically requested an airbed for my comfort. After surgery, I remained in a surreal world, watching nurses and doctors attend to me but not really feeling part of it myself. I welcomed visitors and talked when I could, all in a dream-like state, disassociated from my body.

Later, I awoke in a hospital room. Dr. James was sitting by my side. When I saw him there, so somber and uncertain, I understood how tenuous my future was. With compassion in his voice, Dr. James told me that I could help my body heal. He explained that I could visualize my body as well and healthy and make it so. There were plenty of books on the subject, and he especially suggested I read Dr. Simonton. This messenger was an angel from heaven who would change my life forever.

I sent my sister to get all the books she could find on visualization. I didn't have a clue what my doctor was talking about, but I would learn. My journey had begun. The days following surgery were filled with physical and emotional pain. The pain that was hardest to bear existed in the deepest part of my heart. I hurt for my beautiful children, who were brought into this world to be cared for and guided by me, their mother. But there I lay, in a hospital bed, unable to hold and comfort them.

When the kids arrived for their first visit, they looked perplexed, though they tried to smile and be strong. I saw the fear in their faces when they realized I couldn't move or hold them. However, their natural curiosity made it all bearable. They were inquisitive about everything: my bed, my leg, the nurses and the IV drip. Their trust, faith and love were such gifts to me.

My days in the hospital were filled with visitors. Family, friends, acquaintances, nurses and doctors streamed in daily. Yet no one knew what to say to me. They were uncomfortable, and I felt the pain and sorrow they were feeling. I welcomed their visits and loved talking and listening to the reports of the outside world. It felt so strange: that world was unchanged for them, but it had forever changed for me. I wasn't sure what would be next, but I knew it would be different.

While waiting for the pathology report, Tim and I kept our spirits up and hope alive. We knew the doctors were expecting the worst, even without them saying. My tumor was a Clarks Level II, Stage IIB. We learned there are five levels to Clark's scale. Level II meant the tumor was 1.5mm to 3.0mm in depth. My tumor measured 2.0mm, but that was somewhat inconclusive because of the scarring from previous biopsies.

Staging cancers is typical protocol for any cancer. At that time, there were four stages. Stage IIB meant the tumor had not spread to the lymph system or other organs. However, the doctors didn't know where the tumor had begun. It didn't look like a primary tumor, but there was no evidence of any other disease. They wouldn't really know without further tests. This caused concern and uncertainty for them. Tim and I felt it was good news; at least, it was better than we had expected. In the following years, we would come to understand how naïve we were about melanoma.

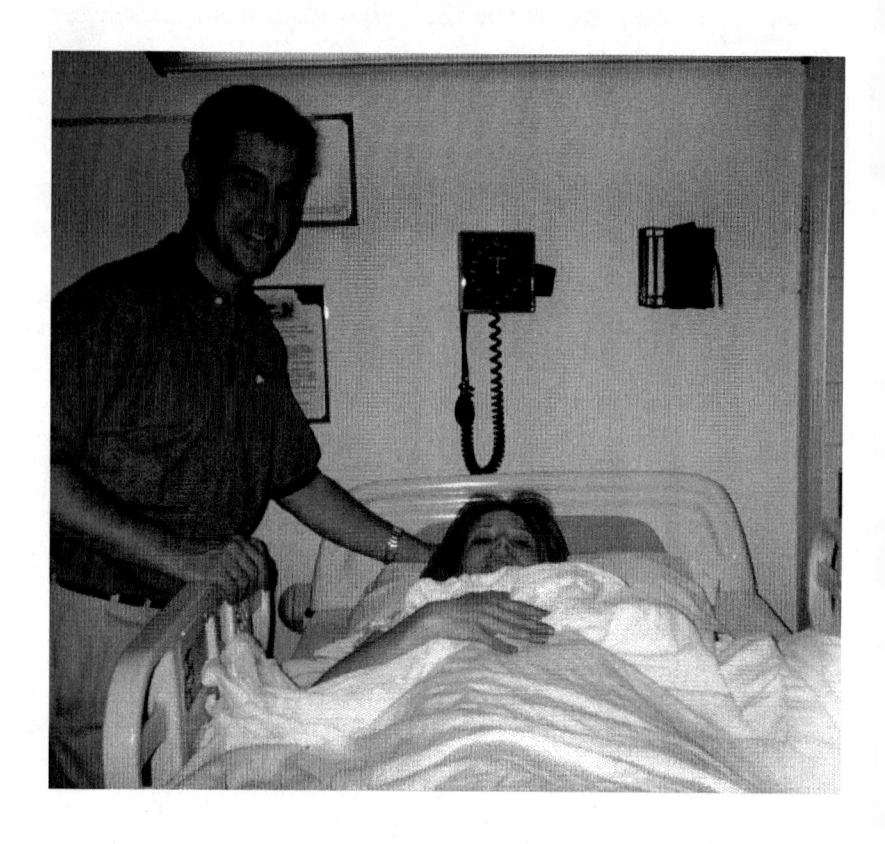

As long as I was in the hospital, I was protected from the demands of the outside world. After my release, the trials became real. We were home again, with all the responsibilities that come with raising three children, including school and all the activities. In addition, I now had another responsibility, to heal and survive. I spent my days in a hospital bed in the living room. I was unable to walk and had to stay as still as possible. Every other day, Tim drove me two hours away to see Dr. James, who would check my progress and clean and redress my wounds.

Still numb by the new realities of our life together, we went through the motions of living. Tim managed our home and the kids while trying to fulfill his responsibilities as a banker. Fortunately, his employer was understanding and gave Tim all the time he needed to take care of his family.

I felt chaos all around me. The phone rang constantly. Everyone wanted to help, to offer love and support. It was wonderful and exhausting at the same time. I could see the mental and physical exhaustion on Tim's face, too. My heart ached with sorrow for the pain I was causing my family.

Each day Tim helped me bathe, carried me to the bathroom and dressed my wounds. I don't know how he looked at that terrible site. When I finally had the courage to look at my leg, I was shocked. It was half the size of the other and looked like a big bruise, with black stitches holding the buttocks skin to my leg. I wanted to vomit.

My buttock was raw and covered with a clear plastic bandage. The site drained, and the bandage was filled with bloody liquid. It was awful to look at and very uncomfortable. In the meantime, our family was trying to live as normally as possible. I can't imagine what my kids must have thought. The past week had been a nightmare for Carlie, Claire and Connor. There had been little time to sit down with them and explain what was happening. They pieced together bits and pieces of overheard conversations, along with the activities they witnessed, and each came to his or her own conclusions.

Dressing My Wounds with Claire

Carlie our oldest daughter, sought escape by continuing her life as normal. Her life was filled with school, skating and friends. Life was all about having fun as a sixth-grader. She participated in some kind of activity every day and never talked about what was happening to the life she once knew.

Expressing feelings had never been easy for Carlie. She found survival easier by blocking out painful emotions. I knew she carried the pain with her each day, and I could feel the stress it was causing her. Tim and I were very concerned about her emotional health and asked her to talk with a school counselor. Adolescence is a difficult time, anyway, and coping with the mortality of her mother was more than she could confront by herself.

Claire, my second born, is a sweet, sensitive spirit, full of compassion and quick to express love. She was a first grade student and learning to read during my early recovery. She would sit by my bedside each day and read a story to me. One day she asked, "Is there no cure for cancer?" A boy in her class had informed her of the "real" meaning of cancer. I explained as much as I thought was appropriate for her, answered her questions and talked about her fears.

Even three-year-old Connor knew something big was going on, although we tried to maintain our typical routine. One evening, while traveling to a school event, Connor spoke with certainty, "You know, if my mom dies, she will always be an angel on my shoulder."

In the early days of my illness, all of our friends and family were available any time we needed them. They prepared and delivered meals four times a week, cleaned our home, drove our children to activities, ironed our clothes, baked bread and cookies. Without all of these loving people, I don't know how we would have survived those first weeks.

Still, the stress of the whole situation was taking a toll on us. I wanted to be involved and help, but I couldn't get up. Tim was scrambling to work each day and coping with the kids at night. We were exhausted physically and mentally. I knew I had to be strong and heal, and I had to help my family. How could I possibly accomplish all this?

Oftentimes the truth is hard to face. My heart ached for my husband and children. I wanted to keep them safe and carry them through this nightmare. I wanted to control their environment and protect them from any more pain. However, this nightmare was part of each of their journeys as much as it was my own. With this experience, they would learn critical life lessons for the growth of their souls, just as I would. They would integrate these lessons and use them to become the best people they could be.

For myself, I never asked why. I knew why. I remembered how crazy life had been just a few months ago. I had known it was out of balance. My priorities were out of whack, although I couldn't tell whether they were upside-down, backwards or nonexistent. I was unconsciously spinning in the wheel of life.

I had tried to use my own human power to balance my life and responsibilities. My spiritual life was low on the priority list, and I wasn't making much progress. The more I tried to change things, the more they stayed the same. At a soul level, I was ready to change my life.

As I lay in bed one night, I surrendered. I prayed that the cycle of busy-ness would stop, that my priorities would be set right, that meaning would be restored to my life. I was willing to go through whatever it took. I would accept it all.

So when the diagnosis came, as terrified as I was, there was a part of me that recognized it as an answer to my prayer. This was my opportunity to be transformed, but with it came a choice.

Before cancer, I was disconnected from who I really am. I had lost my true self in playing the roles of wife, mother, employee, daughter, and friend.. None of these alone was the essence of me. The real me never had a chance to live, so now I was facing death. I had a decision to make. To live didn't mean just changing my old life; it meant facing the death of my old life. I chose to live.

Chapter 2

Doctors, Doctors, Doctors

Those first few weeks after my cancer diagnosis, I existed from one moment to the next. If longing for the innocence and joy of the past six months was painful, thinking about the future was just plain frightening. What was going to happen to me? What about my children? The activity in our home with family and friends distracted me and allowed me to live only in the present moment.

Then the real task began; it was time to determine a course of treatment. Since my tumor was already removed, and there was no current evidence of disease, there was no protocol to follow. I began researching melanoma, its treatments and prognosis. The more I learned, the less I wanted to know. Melanoma is deadly, unpredictable, incurable and basically undetectable. The facts and statistics were dreadful, but I was determined to survive.

Lying in my hospital bed at home, I waited patiently, at first, for a plan from my doctors. I assumed they would arrange a meeting with all the relevant people to establish an action plan. After all, I had an oncologist that specialized in cancer, a dermatologist that specialized in skin and a plastic surgeon that specialized in melanoma and reconstruction. I felt fortunate to have such a good team of doctors, and I was sure they would huddle up and deliver a game plan soon.

I waited and waited. Finally, frustrated and scared, I called my dermatologist, Dr. Kay. She had performed my first biopsy and was the person who gave me the cancer diagnosis. On both occasions, I had found her to be kind and very competent. Dr. Kay and I will both remember that phone call for the rest of our lives. When I learned that there was no plan of action, nor even a meeting set, I realized it was up to me to take charge. I very emphatically told Dr. Kay that I had three small children who wondered if their mother was going to live or die. We didn't have time to wait and think about it. I wanted to live and see my children grow. I wrote a plan and delegated specific tasks to each of my doctors to complete before our meeting, which I set for the next week.

When Tim and I got to the hospital for that meeting, we were anxious to hear my options for treatment. I asked to be directed to the conference room for our meeting and was told they didn't have one. (I found out later that they usually didn't have meetings like this.) So we met in an exam room.

The oncologist began the meeting by explaining that, given the depth of my tumor, there wasn't a clear path of treatment. CAT scans and physical examinations had not located any melanoma in my body at this time; however, the doctors were uncertain if the cancer had attacked the lymphatic system. If so, treatment options were available.

I had four options to choose from, two of them pertaining to the lymphatic system. If the cancer had spread up my left leg into the lymphatic system, the prognosis would be worse and the treatment path could be different. We needed to determine the extent of the disease.

The first option involved removing all of the lymph nodes on the left side of the groin. This could produce undesirable side effects, including swelling in my leg and a compromised immune system. I knew my immune system was vital in fighting this disease. The treatment included major surgery and removing a large mass of skin and tissue. This option was very invasive and aggressive.

The second option, Sentinel Lymph Node Dissection, was just beginning to be used by some oncologists at that time. This procedure identified the main node, or first node in a group of lymph nodes, which indicated the health of the lymph nodes in the area. Radioactive dye is injected where the tumor was. The dye travels through the lymphatic system and progresses to the sentinel node area. The sentinel node is identified using an instrument that measures radioactivity. Then the sentinel lymph node is surgically removed and tested for cancer. This procedure was far less invasive and provided information on the extent of the disease.

The third option for treatment was immunotherapy via an experimental vaccine. A variety of clinical trials were being conducted at this time all over the country.

Tim and I learned a new vocabulary during the course of this meeting. We took notes and had to learn fast. "A clinical trial is a scientific study to determine the safety and effectiveness of a new treatment." "The objective of a vaccination is to introduce a foreign substance to the body and stimulate the body's immune system to attack." "Each melanoma vaccine has a specific composition and each clinical trial tests its effectiveness."

We discussed the various vaccines and the intentions of the studies. Having this conversation was like taking an entire college course in just a few minutes. For each trial, requirements existed for participation. Some required that the disease be at a specific level and stage, while others excluded patients with previous treatments or surgeries. Some studies required the tumor be in the body, while others required evidence of no current tumor in the body. The complexity of it all made me laugh. Could suffering and dying people really sort through all these requirements?

Our fourth option was to do nothing but wait and see. That was a scary thought to me, especially since these same doctors had shown such extreme concern. Therefore, this option was the least desirable. I didn't want to just cross my fingers and hope for the best. I wanted to proactively eliminate the probability of recurrence. I would fight and survive.

The doctors kept saying how happy they were that I was asking questions and actively involved in my care. I didn't understand what they meant. Weren't all patients actively involved in their care? The process, the team, the questions and the comments all seemed odd to me. Slowly over time, the pieces would begin to fall into place.

Now that we knew the options, the next step was to evaluate each one and make a decision. We evaluated vaccination trials from around the country, obtained the most up-to-date medical information from around the world and evaluated each of our team's opinions. Melanoma did not have a good treatment protocol. Many studies were being conducted, but nothing looked promising. It was like choosing the best of the worst.

Our team decided we would choose two programs to evaluate; a vaccination trial at Duke University and a lymph node procedure at M.D. Anderson Cancer Center. Dr. Kay wanted to accompany us to M.D. Anderson in Houston, Texas. I was comforted by her concern and dedication, yet curious about what seemed to be her over-involvement in my case. More would be revealed with time.

We arrived in Houston and checked into our hotel, which was a hotel specifically for patients at M.D. Anderson. The lobby smelled like a sterile hospital. Upon entering, we were confronted by the sight of cancer patients wearing masks to protect themselves from germs in the world around them. In the elevator, we visited with a man in a wheelchair. His head was shaved, and he had stitches encompassing his entire skull. He was pale and sick, and my heart sank. What were we doing here?

Once off the elevator, Tim and I remained silent for several minutes. Then we burst into laughter at the incredible scene we were a part of. What had happened to the world we once knew? We were co-stars in a movie we didn't even want to see.

The next day we met with a surgeon at M.D. Anderson, anxious to hear another option for treatment. After the routine questions and examination, he presented his conclusions. I asked that Dr. Kay be included in our meeting to hear his conclusions. He would not allow it. How could he not allow it? I was his patient; I was paying him! This surgeon was abrupt, arrogant and incredibly rude. He wouldn't let us speak and was belittling when answering our questions. Tim and I were appalled by his behavior. Where was the compassion and concern for us? After reviewing my scans, pathology reports and biopsies, the surgeon informed us we only had one option. We had to remove all the nodes in my left groin through surgery, and I would have drainage tubes and swelling in my leg. He insisted this procedure needed to be done immediately. We knew there were other options and tried to discuss them, including the Sentinel Node Dissection. He rudely told us it was impossible to do this procedure, because my tumor had already been excised. We left his office exhausted, but more determined than ever to fight this disease.

It was on the flight home that I perceived just an inkling of the truth that would set me free. It was February 1995. Tim and I were in an airplane, thirty-thousand feet up in the air, coming home from M.D. Anderson. I sat up in my seat and said to my husband, "This isn't right! All the doctors, nurses and so-called experts are only looking at eliminating the tumor from my body. What about the rest of me?" Then I heard, “Heal the Whole: Body, Mind and Spirit.”

At that moment I didn’t really know what I was trying to say or exactly what it meant. I only knew in my heart and soul that something wasn’t right about the way the medical community approached my healing. At a loss for words, I drew a picture of me – all of me. My body, mind, emotions, and spirit. Looking at my drawing I knew, “This is who I am, not a tumor. I need to heal all of me.

Years later I realized, it was then that I first heard the song of my soul. My inner voice, ignored for so long, was screaming to be heard through this illness. In that moment, I received the message that would save my life. I began the journey to answer the call and recover my whole self.

I understood now that my life depended on me. I was frightened, yet peaceful. I knew God had sent this life-saving message. I opened to God and my soul, and I would listen.

At home, the healing process was exhausting physically, mentally and financially. I was still healing from surgery. My leg was now in a walking brace, to protect the lower leg and skin graft. My buttock was still a bloody, raw sight. Every day we removed the bandage to clean and redress the wound. We had to be extremely careful not to disturb the new skin growth. The donor site was red, and it burned. The healing was incredibly slow. I had an allergic reaction to the antibiotic we were using. What else could possibly go wrong?

Dr. James still cleaned and examined my wounds once per week. On one visit, his nurse inadvertently omitted the lubricating ointment before applying the bandage. Next time the bandage was removed for cleaning, all of my new skin ripped off. I was back to square one again.

Our next step was a visit to Duke University in Durham, North Carolina to evaluate the vaccination program. Durham is very peaceful and beautiful, and Duke University is a beautiful college, set in rolling hills with trees and a spectacular garden. We would meet Dr. Hill at the melanoma clinic at Duke University. Dr. Hill was an eccentric physician who had dedicated his life to the study of melanoma. He had administered his melanoma vaccine for twenty years with great success; however, he would not provide any documentation. The vaccine was administered to all of his melanoma patients, because he didn't believe in double blind studies. His mission was to help everyone with this disease, and he believed his vaccine helped them, so he wasn't interested in giving anyone a placebo. Other professionals in this field did not respect Dr. Hill's studies or his vaccinations. He was a maverick, setting a standard for himself, not following the medical community bureaucracy.

We, too, were uncomfortable with the lack of documentation and Dr. Hill's insistence that we trust his word, but the need to do something set in. We were torn. We evaluated pros and cons. I would have to fly to Duke University once a month for seven long months, get my vaccination and fly home the next day. This decision was a big commitment for our family, but we had to proactively fight this awful disease.

We made the decision to take the vaccine without consulting our team. I never anticipated the effect this decision would have on my family and me. Tim and I returned to Minnesota in hopes of creating as much normalcy as possible for our kids.

Our middle child Claire was struggling in school. She cried every day and wanted to stay home with me. We didn't understand the extent of her fear yet. I was so consumed with healing and survival, little energy was left to deal with my children's emotional needs.

Mom & Claire Trying Hard to Keep Smiling

Connor was only three and seemed content and happy. Grandpa and Grandma spent a lot of time with him, which made every day an adventure for my little boy. They loved and cared for him almost daily and he loved them. He didn't appear to be affected by the chaos around him. It would be years before we saw the effects of trauma he carried within his being.

Carlie had just turned twelve and was still deeply involved with her friends. She thrived on social events and seemed to ignore everything going on at home. But her grades were slipping in school, and we needed help. None of

Carlie's teachers talked to her about this terrifying experience. It seemed everyone was ignoring it, and Carlie was running away.

Meanwhile, more medical decisions were on the horizon. We still did not know the extent of the disease or if melanoma had invaded the lymphatic system. We had to investigate the possibility of a Sentinel Lymph Node Dissection procedure. Through research, we found a doctor at the University of Minnesota who had performed six of them.

Dr. Jack had a completely different perspective than the surgeon at M.D. Anderson. He said I was the perfect candidate for a Sentinel Dissection and felt it was a great option for me. The tumor did not have to be present in my body for the procedure to be successful. This would give us a missing piece of the puzzle: How far had the disease progressed?

Once again I checked into the hospital for a day surgery. Nurses injected a dye into my leg, took pictures, waited, took pictures and waited some more. Then Dr. Jack took me into surgery to find the sentinel node and remove it for biopsy. The procedure went well. He removed the sentinel node and some additional nodes in the area. All of the nodes were negative for melanoma. This was the best news we could have heard. It boosted our spirits and provided us with hope.

Then, just two weeks after receiving the first vaccine, I got sick. I felt pain all over my body, as if I had the flu. I spent the rest of the month in bed. Then I flew to Duke for my second vaccination. When I checked into the hotel a deep loneliness took over. How much longer would this go on? I'm glad I didn't know the answer at that time, or I may have given up right then.

I was excited to go to the clinic the next day. Strange as it may sound, I found comfort in being around others who, like me, were struggling with a deadly disease. The doctors and nurses at Duke specialized in melanoma, so they lived and breathed it every day. I could talk to other patients and ask all those questions that were stored inside.

It was difficult to remember all the information I got during an appointment, so I decided a small tape recorder could save writing time. When Dr. Hill walked in and saw that tape recorder, his face dropped as if I carried a bomb. I tried to explain my simple reasoning, but his attitude said he wasn't buying it. What was he trying to hide? I think many doctors are so paranoid of lawsuits and violating rules, they forget to keep the patient first.

Dr. Hill did allow me to use the recorder but was very careful what he said. I was anxious to hear an explanation of why I had been feeling so sick. He would only say that I must have had a virus or something, which surprised me. I received my second vaccine and flew back to Minnesota.

The month following that second vaccination was worse than the first. I was tired and hurt all over. It was difficult to do the most basic chores. Luckily, at that time I still had a crew of friends and family helping me. Tim was back at work, and the kids were all back in their routines. They all seemed to be coping quite well. I thought I was the only one not coping. I didn't know how to live being sick.

I kept trying to be who I thought I was supposed to be for my family. I didn't understand yet that I would need to take time to learn who I was, just for me. I thought if I kept my attitude as positive as possible, if I was organized and performed my responsibilities as a wife and mother, everything would turn out fine. Isn't that what we have all been taught?

But deep down, I carried the pain of loss, pain for my kids and husband and the fear of death, not to mention the physical pain I was in. I also had pain because I was beginning to lose my connection to other people. People didn't talk to me about my disease or how I was coping, and when they didn't ask I felt they were hoping I wouldn't bring it up. The fear of death affects everyone in some way or another.

Summer came, and I had my first follow-up CAT scan, the big six-month scan! The results were promising, with no evidence of metastatic disease. That was great news, even if I didn't have the energy to participate in fun summer activities. The kids were home for summer vacation, and I found it more and more difficult to be patient in just caring for their basic needs. That was very sad for us all.

Each month I flew to Duke for two days and received my vaccination. The kids were accustomed to this routine already and stayed busy with Grandma. I was sick for the entire summer. It was like months and months of having the flu.

I was anxious for the vaccinations to be done with, thinking I would feel better when we reached the end. September would be my last trip to Duke. Dr. Hill and all of his nurses acted perplexed each time I came to see them. They couldn't understand why I was so sick when no one else had ever had a reaction to the vaccine. I was curious about how they did follow-up with their patients. They suggested I go see a specialist to find out what was wrong with me.

I took their advice, trusting in all they said and did. We found an internal medicine doctor and described everything I was experiencing. He did every blood test for every disease he could think of. He sent me to a neurologist for more tests. We did heart tests, thyroid tests and had a spinal tap for who-knows-what.

On the day of the spinal tap, the doctor had a hard time getting the huge needle into my spine to obtain spinal fluid. Tim was patiently waiting and watching. He had been by my side for every test and exam. Now, the doctor had to pull the needle out and try a second time. Tim's face turned pale, and the doctor asked if he was all right.

After the procedure, I was quite a few steps ahead of Tim as we walked to the parking lot. I stopped and turned around to see what was taking him so long. He was pale and looked exhausted. He said, "I don't know how much more I can take!" He was hitting overload.

All the tests came back "normal," and I was still sick. The internist suggested that maybe I was depressed and needed an antidepressant medication. I didn't really know anything about clinical depression. I said, "Who wouldn't be depressed if they had the flu for five months and had cancer?" We rejected the antidepressant, because we didn't want to add to an already complicated medical case.

We made it through the summer, and the two older kids returned to school, which was a welcome relief for me. While they were in school, I could rest all day and be fresh when they came home. Connor, however, was now just four years old and still home with me each day. We spent many days together in my bed, talking, watching TV and reading.

Connor was a loving and gentle little boy who instinctively knew not to ask for much. He would get his own snacks or help me make lunch and then crawl back into bed with me. He seemed content to stay by my side all day. Later I came to realize this was not contentment, but fear. He did not want to leave my side for fear I would die while he was gone. He did not ask for much in the way of mothering because he didn't want to "kill" me by taxing my strength.

My last trip to Duke finally came in September. Dr. Hill was still quite adamant that something other than the vaccine was making me sick. He claimed that out of 20,000 vaccines he administered, not one person had a reaction like I had. This was hard for me to believe. He suggested that I bypass the last vaccine since I had been so sick (even though he said it had nothing to do with the vaccine). I only wanted to be well, so I agreed to skip it. I was exhausted physically and mentally from being sick for so long. I didn't take the seventh vaccination and was determined to feel better now.

But I didn't feel better. In fact, as the months went by I felt worse.

January 1996 came, and it was time again for the six-month CAT scan. I saw my oncologist, Dr. Barb, a few days after the scans. She thought I was doing well and was very compassionate about my illness. She suggested more than once that the vaccine, being a foreign substance to my body, could cause flu-like symptoms. She was a great listener and always responded with love and kindness. She summarized my scans and was pleased with my overall good health and progress.

Dr. Barb went on to say that I had a cyst on one of my ovaries but that this was quite common in women. Often, she said, the cyst will burst over time. She didn't seem concerned, but I wanted to know more about the cyst, such as its size and location. I will never forget those fingers of hers showing me an orange-sized shape. She said it was nine centimeters in size. I thought, "That is huge!" She casually suggested that I might want to see a gynecologist and have an exam. Then she'd see me in six months.

After a few days, I called to make an appointment with a gynecologist that Dr. Barb recommended. At first, I got an appointment scheduled for the middle of April. That was three months away. "This woman must be good!" I thought. Then I called back and told what I thought was a little white lie. I told the receptionist I had melanoma and that it may have spread to my ovary. To wait three months for an appointment was too dangerous. I got another appointment within days.

Dr. Penny is a beautiful, gentle, compassionate doctor. I loved her right away and trusted her judgment. She suggested, because of my history, that we do a laparoscopy and check out the cyst. That was fine with me, so we scheduled it for two weeks away, February 13, 1996. Dr. Penny also found a suspicious lump in my breast that she wanted to biopsy at the same time. Another doctor joined the team to perform the breast biopsy.

Tim's face fell when I told him I was having surgery again. I wasn't concerned, but he was petrified. He said, "This can't be good!" I assured him everything would be fine and maybe it would alleviate some of the excessive bleeding I had during my periods.

For the third time in my life, I had a general anesthesia. I was becoming a pro. I specifically asked for the "forget it" drug. I loved that drug. I knew I'd receive it on the way to the operating room, and I wouldn't remember a thing.

For some reason, my parents and sisters came to the hospital for that surgery. I don't remember any urgency or extreme worry, but they must have known something I didn't. The surgery went well. The cyst peeled off smoothly. Dr. Penny bagged it and removed it. Immediately afterward, she came to the waiting room and told my family that the cyst looked okay, but she would have to wait for the pathology report to come the next day to be sure.

I went home feeling groggy but confident. By the following afternoon, I was able to move a little. My mom had come to help with the kids and do the laundry. I put on red pajamas and moved to the couch to greet my family with "Happy Valentine's Day!" when they came home.

Instead, I got the second dreadful phone call. It was Dr. Penny, and her speech was hesitant. My heart sank. The cyst was melanoma. The doctor was clearly shaken. She had just gotten the results and was on her way out of town for a few days. She would call when she got home.

I got off the phone screaming and crying. My mom tried to comfort me, but no words could ease my pain. I was sure I would die.

Tim came home to this horrific scene, and we quickly arranged sleep-away parties for the kids. We didn't know what to say to them, so we protected them until we could compose ourselves. Tim and I sat at home for three days and cried. What were we going to do? When would this nightmare end?

When we had no more tears left, we finally developed a plan and began to take one little step at a time. We decided to see a family counselor to help all of us cope with our feelings and address the critical issues we were facing with this disease. We felt that a counseling session might be too much for little Connor, but we took Claire and Carlie with us.

In the counselor's office we gently tried to explain that my disease had progressed and I might need more surgery. The girls were silent. I sometimes try to imagine the fear they must have felt.

Claire had begun to write all her feelings in a journal, so she grabbed my journal and began to write. She sat on my lap in the counselor's office with tears streaming down her face. She could feel the energy around her and knew it wasn't good. She spoke through her tears and expressed her grief with the words of a seven-year-old. I remember how proud I was of her and her brave little soul, speaking her truth.

Carlie is a talented, compassionate, energetic, people person, but she had retreated into a world of her own. At thirteen, she was at a critical stage of development, and we didn't want to lose touch with her. But Carlie's survival skills had kicked in already. She was tough, rebellious and certainly not going to talk to any counselor. The counselor, Tim and I tried every angle to allow Carlie to express her grief and fear. She tucked her legs close to her chest and faced the door, as if she would run at any moment. She wasn't going to talk about anything!

Back in the routine at home, we tried to minimize our fears and anxieties as best we could. Whenever the kids were in school or at friends' houses, we tried to discuss and plan the next chapter of our lives. Dr. Penny returned from her trip and had already recruited a surgical oncologist to assist her.

Because it is actually rare for melanoma to spread to the ovaries, there were varying opinions on the extent of hysterectomy needed. Dr. Penny and the surgical oncologist consulted with various doctors around the country, and the consensus was to remove as much as possible. They knew the melanoma cells were free to grow in my abdomen.

Tim and I also spent a few hours with a local melanoma specialist, Dr. Tom, to obtain more information, options and future treatment alternatives. At this point, the doctors believed I was probably in the later stages of cancer and that the melanoma had spread to my intestines, uterus, lymphatic system, and throughout my abdomen. Of course, they didn't tell us this at the time, but they didn't have to. Each meeting and each call I had with any of my doctors, their faces and voices said it all.

By this time, my dermatologist Dr. Kay and I had become friends and frequently spoke over the phone. I called her immediately after receiving the news of metastatic melanoma. She panicked! She tried hard to compose herself, but I knew she was struggling. I didn't understand at the time why she was taking this so personally. I knew I was her first melanoma diagnosis, but I didn't understand why she was so attached.

Later, I came to understand that Dr. Kay is a derma-pathologist who mainly conducts business in her lab, studying tissue samples and then reporting on findings. She worked in a clinic setting two days per month just to stay close to patients, to see and touch the skin that she usually observed under a microscope. I was her first patient from whom she removed melanoma cells, studied them and made a diagnosis. It took awhile for me to understand this whole picture. Dr. Kay had seen thousands of melanomas in the lab, but I was her first patient with melanoma.

Dr. Kay didn't believe the ovarian cyst was melanoma. She was trying hard to convince herself that this could not happen and told me to hold on before acting too fast. I learned later that she went in search of my tumor, the biopsies and the pathology reports. She was going to see this for herself. After reading all the reports and looking at the biopsy, Dr. Kay still wasn't convinced it was metastatic melanoma. The tumor cells were very unusual, and they had not determined the primary tumor site.

Meanwhile, I was advised by others to proceed with surgery. I was confused and so were my doctors. This was not a good feeling. I always thrived on structure and order, but it seemed like everyone was falling apart.

Of course, I was into the books and research papers learning all I could. I thought I had to keep up with the doctors to make sure they did the right thing. This was ridiculous in one way, but paid off in others. I found out, for instance, that the tumor had to be processed in a certain way if it was going to be used in any studies.

Right away, I was on the phone with my doctors asking about their procedures for processing tumors and preserving them for future studies. They didn't have a system for preserving the tumor, so I directed them to people I had contacted on the east coast to assure my tumor would be safe. At this point I knew there were other vaccinations available for my new level of disease, and we had to be prepared for the future.

Tim and I decided that the only surgery that made sense was a total hysterectomy – the removal of ovaries, tubes, uterus and cervix. Anything related to the reproductive system was suspect and had to be removed. Moreover, the doctors decided on exploratory surgery to determine how far the disease had spread. They would open me up and feel every inch of my intestines for tumors, look for any tumor in the liver, remove aorta lymph nodes for biopsy, and search the abdomen for any other evidence of disease. That sounded fine with me at this point. I was so numb from the whole experience I would agree to almost anything that might help.

It had only been one week since my last surgery, and I was back again. I was in amazingly good spirits and wasn't really afraid. A built-in mechanism that shields us from trauma had kicked in. My sisters came to send me off to surgery, along with Tim and Dr. James.

Dr. Jan was the new member of the team, a surgical oncologist who had performed a similar surgery a few years prior. She would perform the surgery along with Dr. Penny. I received the "forget it" drug and off I went to sleep. After the surgery, Penny and Jan told my family they found suspicious tissue in both ovaries and the uterus.

When my eyes opened again, the pain was incredible. I had been told I would have an auto-morphine valve I could use when I needed it for pain. I never received an auto-valve and the pain was difficult to handle and manage. That evening after everyone left, I lay in my bed unable to move, with the pain worsening, the woman in the bed next to me screaming, and all I could do was cry. It felt as if a knife was in my gut, turning and slicing my flesh. I wanted to escape but didn't know how. I was at the mercy of doctors, nurses and this ugly disease.

In addition, I was told my intestines became almost paralyzed from being touched in surgery. When they woke up, the pain was unbearable and took over my whole being. For a while, I truly thought it might kill me. I felt alone, especially at night. It was dark and no one was around to help. It took two hours for someone to respond to my call.

One night as I laid in the darkness of my room, a nurse came in to check my IV and saw I was having a reaction to the morphine. They pulled the IV out and had to start a new one. The nurse used my other arm and tried to insert the IV needle in my forearm. My veins rolled. I tried telling her where my good veins were, but she didn't listen. She tried again and failed. By the third time, I was crying and told her to "Leave right now!"

From that moment on, I felt I had to look out for myself. This was a pattern I'd practiced since I was a child. When surrounded by people who didn't know what to do, I'd do it myself. Later in my recovery, I would learn that I could receive help from other people, people who would listen and were safe, people who had wisdom to share. But that is just one of the many lessons cancer has taught me.

Life in a hospital is a whole other world. I felt far away from everything and everyone. I got updates on the kids, but it all seemed so far away that it was hard to be a part of that world. Carlie, Claire and Connor came to the hospital to see me, once again carrying as much strength as they could find within themselves.

We laughed and made plans for the future. Everyone laughed at me because of my morphine-induced state. I didn't care. I was making plans to take my kids to "heaven on earth." We were going to the Caribbean Sea as soon as I was able. I began to realize my time here may be short, and I was going to spend it with my family in peace and fun.

Trip to the Sea

Trip to Big Mountain in Montana

Trip to Disney World

It was crisis time again, and family and friends streamed in to the hospital to see me. I love my family and all my friends. They felt so much pain and sorrow for our family that they needed to come and be a part of it, too. Everyone helped with the kids, trying to keep them occupied and focused on anything but cancer. My oncologist, plastic surgeon, dermatologist and gynecologist all visited, trying to bring words of encouragement. They were as scared as I was, I think. The nurses became concerned that I wasn't getting enough rest for healing, and they cut off all my visitors.

Finally the pathology report was delivered, and Dr. Penny was pleasantly surprised. The melanoma had spread down one of my fallopian tubes and all other organs and nodes were clean. The news was better than expected.

Now, I had to concentrate on healing. I needed to eat well and not do any work at all. This was a difficult requirement, considering I had three kids at home who needed a mom. Dr. Penny told me I had a great attitude and was incredibly strong after everything I had been through. She told me my strong faith and attitude could alter the course of this disease.

Again, loved ones came to help with the household duties and meals were delivered each day. I still couldn't eat because of the terrible pain in my gut. Two weeks went by. I had lost so much weight that I knew something was wrong.

One evening, I reached an on-call doctor, and she told me I had been through such a traumatic experience that it was normal to feel depressed. I was so miserable I couldn't eat, think or talk. I listened and accepted what she said.

I also noticed my incision getting redder and redder and inquired about the possibility of an infection. Nobody listened. Then one day my incision popped open, and I knew I was in trouble. Off to the doctor again, and this time they believed me. I was so angry with all these professionals who wouldn't listen to me. Clearly, the issue of making myself heard was going to be key to my recovery.

The doctor used pressure on my incision to release the infection from my body. Tim's eyes were huge! He said it looked liked yellow and green cottage cheese. They later found I had acquired a staff infection from the hospital. All I could think and say was, "Just one more thing for my body to fight!" My body had been talking to me for a long time, and I hadn't listened, but it was getting my attention now. Slowly, as the infection healed, I began to eat.

While in bed those first weeks after surgery, I spent a lot a time alone, analyzing my life and this world. I thought of all the pain and suffering people go though, and it made me sad. I wanted to understand life and death at a deeper level.

My soul was leading me to the next step of my healing journey.

There were so many unknowns, but I began to formulate a plan, starting with what I knew. I knew I was potentially facing death. I knew I wasn't ready to die. I knew I had to be aggressive in fighting this disease. I knew my body, mind and spirit were connected. I knew I had to address each one separately and as a whole. I knew I had to act fast.

I studied the clinical trial data again and decided the best chance for survival involved another vaccination. This time I had a tumor waiting in storage on the east coast to be used for an autologous vaccination. An autologous vaccine is one that uses your own tumor cells in the creation of the vaccine. The theory is that your body can better identify its own melanoma cells and set your immune system into action to kill them.

Of course, some doctors said the tumor was removed and there was no evidence of disease, so there was no need for vaccine. After reading the pathology report that stated my tumor consisted of approximately six hundred million melanoma cells and had a high mitotic rate, I wondered how those doctors could possibly believe they scooped out each one of those microscopic cancer cells.

We met with Dr. Tom again to discuss the alternatives for treatment. The autologous vaccine was an option along with

Interferon, an immunotherapy drug, chemotherapy or any combination. He explained that once melanoma spreads to an internal organ there is a very high chance it will recur in a vital organ eventually. Dr. Tom recommended Interferon treatment as his first choice and chemotherapy/Interferon combination as his second choice. On March 11, 1996, Dr. Tom stated, "You will be dealing with melanoma again sooner rather than later!"

Another vaccine was the best option for us. When we contacted Harvard to initiate the vaccine program, though, we learned that my tumor was infected with bacteria and could not be used to create a vaccine. I was devastated! I thought this was my one chance and now my chance was gone because of a bacteria introduced from the hospital.

With the personal vaccine no longer an option, all of my doctors recommended Interferon as our next best option. Tim and I studied the clinical trial data. Interferon was a new drug and was going to become the standard protocol for melanoma. The data we reviewed was haunting. A lot of the patients dropped out of the study due to severe reactions. Others had liver damage, a couple died and the rest were quite sick for the entire year on the drug. The probability of it keeping me alive a little longer didn't compare to the side effects and quality of life. We did not want to try Interferon. If I had a year or two to live, I did not want to have my kids watch me lie in bed sick every day for those last months. I wanted to live life.

Without much discussion on my part, our kids were always aware of the status of my health. One day I was making lunch when I overheard Claire and Connor talking. My four and seven year olds were discussing the ramifications of their mother's death. They finally said to me, "Mom, if you die and Dad gets married again that means we'll have a stepmom, right?"

My children had questions, and they needed answers. I listened and answered all their questions. They were sad, but they were realistic. We always answered their questions and comforted their fears. We never really know the fear they carry and how it will affect their lives in the future. I hoped and prayed that I could help them discard the fear now, so their pain wouldn't show up in their future.

One of my doctors was furious when I rejected Interferon. I explained how we felt about my quality of life and the importance of normalcy within our family. I said that I had been striking out with the medical field, and I needed a new approach. I did not want to live my last days or years in pain. He told me, "Well, the medical field had a bad picture with you to start with!" That was all I needed to hear.

Chapter 3

Growing Up, Not In

Flashing within my mind was the message I had receive on the airplane. "Heal the whole, body, mind and spirit!" Was this a clue? The message so profound and I had neglected was back. I now knew this was my path, my truth. Where had this knowledge come from? I wanted to have regular access to the truth. I had lost my truth, the knowingness from within, some time during my thirty-five years. Where had it gone? How would I find it? I set out on a journey to heal my body, mind and spirit.

Fear crept in to remind me I didn't know how to do it. My analytical brain asked for all the pieces of the puzzle and a list of each step required to accomplish this enormous task of saving my life. Where do I start? Who can help me? Who should I talk to? Does anyone want to hear? "Have faith and it will be," the knowing answered from within. So I set out to understand the beliefs, thoughts and behavior that led to this critical point in my life. This led me back to the beginning.

I was born the fourth of six children. My superficial memories of life as a small child in Minnesota seemed ordinary. I remembered feeling happy and free, curious but cautious, yet somehow uncomfortable. Uncomfortable about what? I continued to search within for the answers to the questions that surfaced.

What I found was that I was simply responding to the energy in my childhood home and the relationships there, like all of us do. That energy didn't feel good. I didn't fit. I withdrew into my head. I came to rely on the power of my thinking brain.

With so many children came a feeling of constant activity in our home. When I think of it now, I can still feel the sense of restlessness that was so unsettling to me as a child. I needed order, even as I longed to be part of the gang.

As a young child, I was free, talkative, spirited, and curious about my world. I was also naturally affectionate. My parents were distracted and busy, and I longed for a real connection to them, especially my mother. I pursued her love, her touch and her attention. I wanted to be close to her, to sit on her lap and drink of the pure love that is the natural home of every child. Those around me perceived these acts of love quite differently. They saw me as a baby and a spoiled brat. My older siblings couldn't see who I was. To them, I was different.

I wanted to feel connected to them, too. I became determined to prove them wrong. "I am not different. I love them and will fit in, and they will love me one day." I withdrew into my head and squelched that loving spirit. I quit reaching out to give and receive love, and I began to use my head to seek approval instead.

Every family has a major theme that it lives by, a reason for being. In some homes, the focus is on spiritual growth and joy. Others are about material acquisition. Some families make it their purpose to train its members to be of service to the world they live in. Our family's theme was basic survival.

My mother's pride and work ethic were strong. This strength propelled her to positions in a company other woman envied. These were the things that defined her. Her love for her family was unspoken. We knew she loved us very much, but the words were few. She, too, had been raised in a home with lots of hard work and little emotion. When survival is the theme for one generation, it tends to be the theme for the next and then the next, until someone does the healing work that breaks the cycle.

My father had grown up as the oldest of three children. His father never accepted him, not even on his deathbed. I can only imagine how much pain that rejection caused him. My father was a maverick, too free to conform, yet always looking for acceptance. His heart is filled with love for others, but it seemed his wounds made it hard for him to accept love. My mother is a survivor and provider. They each have their own paths in life, but they worked hard at keeping their paths parallel for many years.

For both of my parents, every moment of every day was about providing shelter, food and clothing for their six children. For most of my childhood, my mother worked long hours both in-and outside the home. She juggled it all and provided well for our large family, but the focus was on activity and tasks. She was too overwhelmed with these to give any time or thought to feelings and relationships. At a very young age, I developed the core belief that my success in life was defined by how much I could do and how well I could do it.

I formed another crucial belief during a snowy February morning. I was four years old. I was sitting at the breakfast table with my sister Pam, who was five, when she suddenly fell over and started vomiting. She was rushed to the hospital, and for a while no one was sure what was wrong with her. I don't recall anyone talking to me about what happened, but somehow I knew she might have died. It felt as if I was in an isolated shell, watching but not being heard. My life changed that day in a significant way. As the youngest in the family at that time, I went to stay at my grandparent's house while the rest of the family went to the hospital. I had never been left there by myself before. I stared out through a second story window for hours. I felt abandoned and deserted by the people I loved most in this world. I heard someone say the roads were closed, because it was snowing so much. I watched the snow drifting by my window and believed I would never see my family again. I was panicked, alone, stranded. I cried for two days before someone finally took me home. It was too late for an explanation to sooth my aching heart. I was terrified. From that day forward my family called me "Babe."

My sister had been diagnosed with spinal meningitis and survived a life threatening condition, but no one told me that then. I didn't really understand what had happened to my sister. Once I was settled at home with my sister and family, I was happy again.

So where did my loneliness and fear of abandonment go? They went into the combination of factors that shapes a person's development. They would play a big role in my future survival skills. Perhaps not everyone is fortunate enough to uncover and acknowledge those feelings, but cancer gave me the opportunity to heal and make those survival tools obsolete.

To survive in my family, instinct said I had to fit in. My survival skills told me independence was the key. Yet the family myth was that I was different than my siblings. I didn't know then that no matter how self-sufficient I became, they would always see me as the one that had received more than they did. It was like a contest in my family to see who had gotten by on the least amount of love and support. Perhaps because my very young requests for help reminded them too painfully of their own unanswered needs, they had to believe they were different from me. And I didn't know any better than to try to be as self-sufficient as they thought we should be. And to be self-sufficient I had to use what everyone seemed to value about me the most, my brain.

It was true that I was logical and could think through most problems. I came to believe I could use my brain to succeed at anything. I used it to be the best in all subjects in school. My brain was my best friend in those days, and I ignored my heart. My big heart didn't get me very far with my family, but my brain took care of me. As the years went by, I moved through life with plenty of certainty but little feeling.

I did keep some slender threads of connection to my emotions, though. I found comfort in my sister Pam and our neighborhood friend, Kay. We filled our days with adventure and laughs. We rode our bicycles all over town, created forts, talked about life, and just loved each other as we were. True to our training, none of us ever voiced this love, but we all knew that we loved each other.

Playing freely with Pam and Kay was the closest I came to revealing my true self. Our time together was my escape from my home and family, that world where I didn't belong. Our friendship gave all of us hope and joy.

At home, I took part in the constant flurry of activity, but I felt non-existent and invisible. I lived with a veil over my body and soul, protecting myself from the fear of loneliness. If I danced to their song, I thought, I could earn their love. Still, I was singled out as "different" from the rest of them.

I finally understood why my siblings treated me this way when I came to realize this was just one side effect of growing up in a dysfunctional home. Even though it felt so personal, it was never really about me. I retreated even further into my mind and became more determined to survive independently.

All people have a need to belong and feel loved. When that need is not met in our first families, we search for love in other people or activities. This seems to be part of everyone's journey, because no family can meet all of our needs. We live in a world that says happiness lives in activities, things, and people. The truth is that happiness lives in each of us. It is always available.

Like generations before them, my parents were focused on surviving, but they couldn't completely squelch the desire to get more out of life. However, since they only knew how to live in survival mode, their needs for true satisfaction were expressed in other ways. Overwork, alcohol abuse, and relationship
problems were just symptoms of a deeper spiritual hunger to be truly happy. If my parents could have allowed themselves to want more than survival, if they had consciously decided on a different theme for their marriage and family, perhaps they could have had a happier life. Their symptoms distracted them from the true joy available within them and their children. They were too consumed with shame, blame and compulsion to participate in our activities or our inner feelings, much less find joy in them. No one asked about our feelings, yet a piece of me still wanted that connection to my heart. Slowly, with time, I forgot and the veil grew thicker.

I attended a local parochial school until junior high. I was a bright student. There were plenty of friendly kids in school, but I never felt connected to anyone special, perhaps because

I was always so focused on striving to be number one in the class. I remember wanting to be part of the group or to have a very best friend to share all my deep secrets, but I didn't yet know that I was the one who kept that from happening.

As a seventh grader, I entered public school for the first time, and a new group of friends awaited me. From across the hall, I had my eyes fixed on a young man I didn't know. There was an instant curiosity within me. I watched him from a distance that whole year without ever speaking to him. I didn't understand the attraction at the time, but I always knew when he was around. His name was Tim. He was a farm boy, an athlete and a focus of attraction for many junior high girls.

Some people walk into our lives and we have an instant connection. We seem to know them from somewhere and want to be near them. As eighth graders, Tim and I were assigned to the same table in the same homeroom. Our friendship began at that moment. Our first date came when I invited him to a Sadie Hawkins dance and he graciously accepted. Tim touched a piece of my heart that had been starved for a very long time.

At fourteen years old, we connected at a level neither one of us completely understood. We spent Friday and Saturday evening together for many years. Throughout this time, our relationship blossomed into genuine love.

The words we spoke were simple, not deep life truths, but we existed in an energy field of complete comfort. We shared high school games, dances, parties and movies. I became a member of his gang. His buddies accepted me with respect. I belonged. I felt loved and needed, as if part of a family for the first time.

Slowly, I drifted away from my girlfriends. They were experiencing life as teenagers, but I disconnected from their activities and fun. Because of my need for significance and love, I attached my identity to Tim and his life. When I was away from Tim, I felt incomplete. In my mind, the risk of losing other relationships was worth the connection and love I had with Tim. We were so young and yet so committed to each other.

A wonderful friend named Robyn walked into my life in junior high. She was quiet but bold. She was a gentle spirit with a heart of love. We developed an affectionate openness I hadn't experienced since being a young child. We talked for hours about life as I revealed my true self to her. Our hearts connected, and we truly wanted to share ourselves with each other.

Robyn's family had a degree of warmth I had never experienced in a family, and I was comfortable at their home. At the time, I didn't understand the feeling, but I knew it felt wonderful. As I spent more and more time with Tim, however, I neglected Robyn.

My time in high school might have looked happy to outsiders, but a silent observer inside me was unfulfilled. There was a truth locked inside me trying to be heard, and I covered it up. I dealt with this incongruence with a type of boldness and aloofness. I suspect my classmates and teachers saw me as snotty, closed and a little scary. I remember being a silent observer with little expression. So much was hidden inside me, but I refused to let it out.

I never felt quite good enough. I wasn't pretty enough or nice enough or athletic enough or smart enough. I created many experiences to match those beliefs. I was the seventh out of six homecoming attendants. I was the seventh of six starting volleyball players. I was valedictorian of my class yet never inducted into National Honor Society. It was never my fault. "How could they do this to me?" Now I see how I created my reality.

I did graduate at the top of my class, though, which was a goal I set as a junior high student. I was disciplined and focused and had no doubt my goal would be achieved. I used that stubborn determination to prove my family wrong about me.

My older siblings had determined early on that I was a spoiled baby. They continually told me I was given everything, which sent a message to me that I should work harder and do more. The cycle continued to be fed and I allowed it. I didn't realize no prize could have made them see me differently. They needed a scapegoat for the pain in our family, and I was it.

College was upon me, and I struggled to find direction. I wanted someone to guide me, but that guidance wasn't there. I was so alone and confused. My relationship with Tim continued, but I sensed he wanted more freedom. Eager to please him to avoid abandonment, I settled on a college about an hour away from his. Robyn, my best friend was with me, but my neglect of our friendship had taken its toll. Our relationship was no longer as open and loving as it once was. The loneliness and abandonment surfaced again. I didn't fit anywhere.

With Tim unavailable, the search for the next solution began. Alcohol became a regular part of my life in college. It seemed to open up a part of me I'd been searching for – the part that was free, spontaneous, creative, unlimited and verbal. When I drank I became someone I recognized and loved. Feelings, thoughts and knowledge that had been locked away for years spilled out when I was using.

The party always came to an end, though, and I was trapped in the life I had created for myself. I had a lot of fun, but abundant peace and contentment were missing. I wanted to have a different kind of experience, so I began setting goals for my future.

I also began to look to religion to fill the void. I read and studied the Bible for the first time in many years. I took time to be quiet and go within, trying to understand the peace and joy I longed for.

Of course, I had grown up in a parochial school and learned Catholicism. I had recited prayers and participated in the rituals but never truly connected to the spirit of God. As a young girl I thought, "This can't be the only way to heaven. No God would condemn his own creation." I knew truth, but never consciously acknowledged its existence.

I felt lost and was searching. I would read the Bible but couldn't make sense of it. I would visit churches but didn't find it there, either. I immersed myself in school and parties, but always knew there was something more. There were glimpses of my heart opening only to be shut by the outside world around me. So I'd close my heart and conform.

Throughout our college years, Tim and I drifted apart. He wanted freedom and I wanted love and connection. We each had brief relationships with others, but always found comfort in each other's arms. We had a deep connection that we still didn't completely understand. After spending nine months apart, we reunited and committed our lives to each other. One year later, we got married and then graduated from college. We set out to create the life of our dreams.

Chapter 4

Living The Dream

Creating the life of our dreams began prior to our marriage. We often talked about what we wanted most in life and dreamed big dreams as teenagers.

Our graduation from college was our first goal accomplished during our first year of marriage. We worked hard to finish our degrees while working multiple jobs to pay our bills. Upon graduation, we were excited to start the next phase of our life together, moving into true adulthood and entering the professional career world. However, due to economic conditions at the time, the job market was weak and not many offers were given to graduates. Of course, we saw it as an opportunity to travel and have some fun before settling into a life of responsibility.

The week after graduation we packed our car and headed up the Alaskan Highway. Driving through British Columbia and the Yukon, I was completely surprised to see the desolate regions of North America. I repeated several times, "Who lives in the middle of nowhere?" The vegetation, mountains, streams, rivers and lakes were absolutely breathtaking. Camping, talking and laughing we made our way to Anchorage Alaska after two weeks.

Anchorage was quite a vibrant city offering all the services and most luxuries you find in other cities. After staying with a friend for a couple days, we headed to our final destination. Little did I know at that time where I was REALLY going!

We boarded a plane and headed three hundred miles directly west to a small Eskimo/Indian village called Aniak. We hit the runway with a thud, the plane shaking and rumbling with bags falling. Stepping onto the runway, I saw the source of our rough entry, a gravel runway. I looked around and felt as if I had flown back in time.

I couldn't see much of anything in the near distance. Small huts, few trees, and a rundown tin building, they called the terminal, welcomed us. Unbelievable, was the only word that described it. We were welcomed by Dave and Gloria, friends of Tim's family, who were longtime residents of Aniak. They had an apartment in their home we would rent.

Headed to our new home in a pickup truck, I got my first peek at the real adventure awaiting us.

Rushing past us on a three-wheeler was a family of four, one body stacked upon the other. Speechless still, I observed in disbelief. The town was scattered with buildings, or what we would have called shacks. They pointed out the local grocery store, city hall, post office, and various other buildings that service this little remote village. Exhausted and overwhelmed, I remained quiet until the truck stopped. We drove up to a beautiful two-story log home with a balcony and small apartment on the second floor which was our newhome.

Tim had visited one summer before and was quickly catching up on all the new developments with Dave and Gloria. Evening came and I realized the light of day never diminished. I fell into bed hoping I would wake up and the entire experience would look and feel better.

Adjusting to life in the Bush (rural Alaska) was a real challenge for me. The hustle and bustle of city life for the past four years was the norm for me. In Aniak, silence was the norm. Hunting and fishing were the way of life. Tim was busy right away with projects and fishing and all the other things men do. I spent a lot of time alone in the apartment. I quickly found out the mosquitoes ruled the village in the summer. I was unable to leave the house without coating layers of oil on exposed skin.

We spent the summer exploring, fishing and learning to relax. We played cards and cribbage and other quiet games at night; quite different from our college days partying with our friends in the city. Tim began working with the local fishermen guiding tourists along the local rivers. This took him on some great adventures, but left me alone with no TV r radio. Books became my companions.

Shortly after arriving in Aniak, I began feeling ill and fatigued and suspected I may be pregnant. No doctors, no family, no friends, and an absent husband, left me feeling quite lonely. Once again the same feelings of loneliness and abandonment were resurfacing.

Coping with a new environment and the thoughts of becoming a parent, I had no one to reach out to and feel safe. Spending most days alone, I wanted to runaway from the fear I was feeling inside. Instead, I stuffed them away never looking at the pain I really felt inside. I had to find a doctor or someone to help me. In a small building on the edge of town, I found the Aniak Clinic. Inside I found a practicing health aide who agreed to try a pregnancy test. I don't think she had ever done this before. Hours later I found out I was carrying a new life inside me. Unsure of what to do or say, I wandered back home. In seven months, Tim and I would have a new baby and we were excited. A new stage of life was beginning for us, and we were overwhelmed with excitement and uncertainty.

The next few months my mind was overloaded with thoughts of motherhood and what next. I busied myself with reading, cooking, and baking. I loved to read and was learning how one survives in bush Alaska. Because of the remote location of Aniak, most of our groceries were ordered in cases and shipped from Anchorage. We had no fresh produce or bakery goods, so I became the baker of bread, pies and pastries. Quite a role change, from who I thought I was. I became who I thought I was supposed to be. Still believing activities defined me, I set out to fit in this isolated village.

Many questions surfaced for me during this time. I was trying to figure out what I was really doing here. Was this where I wanted to live and raise a child, or was this where Tim wanted to be? It was painful to watch him leave each day for a new adventure, while I was sick and confined to this small apartment. The smoke houses in the summer were nauseating with various fish smells, and the mosquitoes outside were intolerable. I wasn't familiar with all these emerging feelings and didn't know what to do with them. I buried them deeper!

At twenty weeks pregnant, the nausea and fatigue left me. I began babysitting two children from the village to fill my days. Winter came quickly in October and was cold and dark for nineteen hours a day. I was thrilled to feel my baby moving within me. This new life was dependent on me. I felt healthy and strong, but yearned to see a doctor to monitor the baby's progress. Maybe even get a picture of this miracle. I wanted to make plans to get to Anchorage to be sure our child was healthy and safe. Finally in November, six months pregnant, I flew to Anchorage for an appointment with a doctor.

Deprived from some of the basics we take for granted, I was thrilled to shop and explore the real world again. The fourth day, I arrived at the clinic and was told the doctor was snow bound in a village and was unable to see me. I was devastated! How could this happen? Yet again, I buried my disappointment and sadness and boarded the plane back to Aniak.

The following month, I began to plan the delivery of our first child. Since I didn't have a doctor, I was free to deliver wherever I wanted. We had to leave Aniak one month prior to my due date, because if there was an emergency there was no way out of the village. We decided to fly back to Minnesota in January, spend time with family and friends and have our child there.

February 22, Carlie Ann was born healthy and beautiful. What an incredible experience, bringing new life into the world. We bundled her up and headed back to Aniak when she was twelve days old. Carlie was happy and content and experienced airports, airplanes, and snowmobile rides by the time she was two months old. We loved her with all our hearts and were excited to experience the world with her.

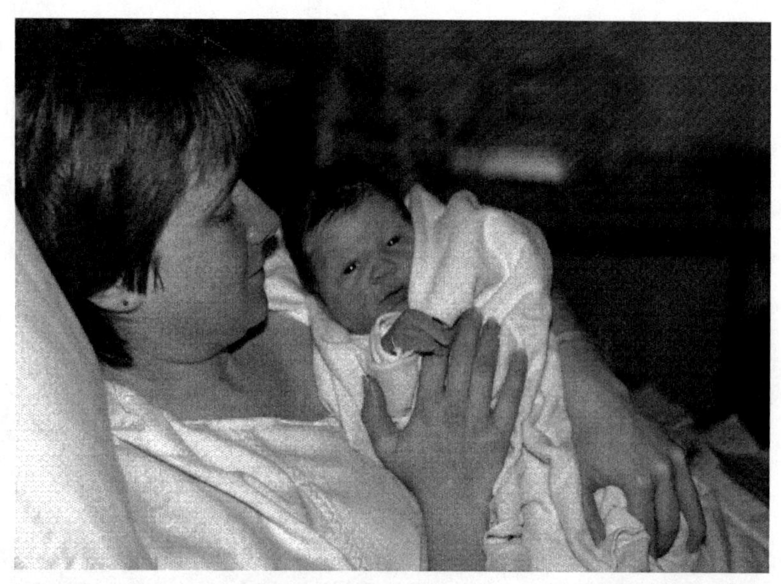

I don't think I really knew who I was, but felt I was back to the Sheila I had known for twenty-three years. Feeling isolated during my pregnancy, I was ready to explore this village we now called home. I was offered a job at the City of Aniak as the treasurer and rode to work on a three-wheeler along the Kuskokwim River. My responsibilities included biweekly payroll and handling all financial statements, including all state grants. The first personal computers were being introduced at this time and through state money we obtained a truckload of equipment. I had never seen a PC before, but I was responsible for automating the City of Aniak's financial processes. In a wooden shack in the middle of nowhere, I was automating an Eskimo village.

After one year in Aniak, we made a decision to move back to Minnesota to raise our daughter. The conditions in Aniak were too remote and did not offer the social, educational, emotional, or cultural environment we wanted for Carlie.

Back to the real world, Tim and I began our careers. We settled in Hutchinson, Minnesota to provide a smaller community environment to raise our family. Tim began his career in banking and I was pursuing mine at a large manufacturing plant focusing on quality and productivity improvement projects.

We believed the opportunities for us were unlimited and continued setting and reviewing ours goals for the future.
We didn't yet know that those thoughts and feelings set into motion the creation of our future reality. We had not yet learned that what we feel, think and say creates our experiences. We were innocently practicing the laws of the universe.

Working in the real world in a career I had always dreamed of was inspiring. I was learning so much about business and how to create quality and teamwork in a manufacturing environment. I became consumed with the thoughts of succeeding professionally, knowing I had the intelligence to be anything I wanted. Through many experiences in the corporate world I learned painful lessons of authenticity. I was so cut off from my emotional self, I was unaware of my words and behaviors and how they affected others. It was difficult to play the games in the corporate world. Logic and fact ruled my entire being.

Messengers along my journey stopped me in my tracks for a moment, and I began questioning who I really was and what I had come here to do. I was unaware of how I was really being and saw so many lessons from a victim's viewpoint. Someone was always responsible for what happened and how I felt. I didn't remember that all these feelings were my internal guidance system telling me I was not aligned to who I was or what I wanted. So I kept doing more and more activities to prove my worthiness.

I worked long hours and then continued my work at home, raising our daughter, maintaining a home and fulfilling social responsibilities Tim and I had taken on. I was proud of the juggling I was doing and was convinced I could do it by Tim and my family role models. I switched hats several times a day with all the roles I was playing in life. Over time I could feel the physical and mental strain I was creating. I felt as if I could never do enough no matter how many hours were in a day. But I was determined to keep trying.

Carlie was growing up fast and we began talking about having another child. I knew I was already busy, but deeply wanted another child too. Again, I tried to reevaluate my priorities, but work and all my responsibilities got in the way. Claire Marie was born five years after Carlie and we were again amazed at the miracle of life. Our hearts were bursting with love and admiration for this bundle of joy.

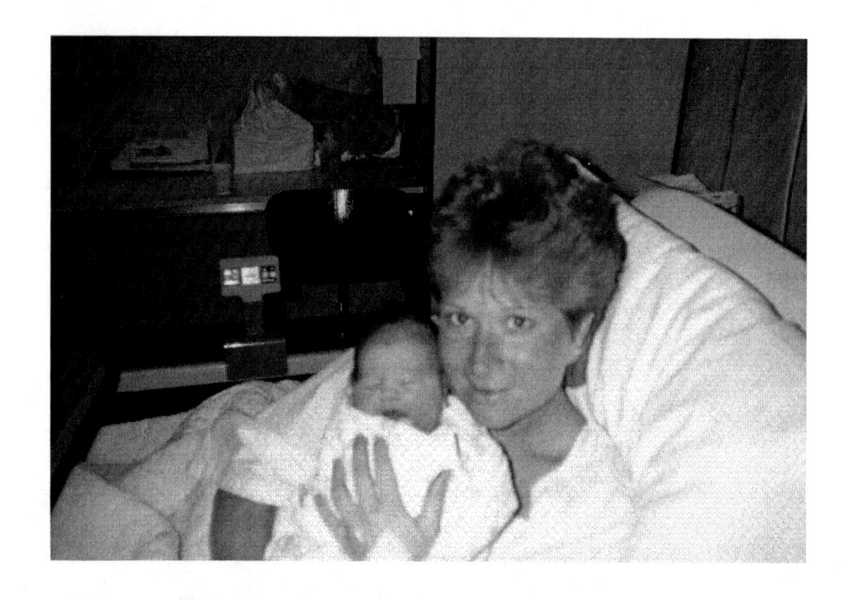

Now the challenge was even bigger! Two children and their activities, a home to maintain, two careers, and community and social responsibilities, all became part of the juggling game. Once again I proved to myself I could do anything I put my mind to. Although many times I was overwhelmed and tired, I didn't know how to quit doing what I was doing. Buried deep in my suitcases of life was my core belief I continued to live by. I believed my success in life was defined by how much I could do and how well I could do it.

But, we had a life plan and we were on track. Our family was the top priority and we wanted to experience life together. The plan included financial goals, a new home, traveling, a lake home, family golf and skiing. We were creating what we wanted in life. And life was fun! We were involved in many community and family activities that we celebrated together. Some of our most memorable times included camping in northern Minnesota. We golfed and skied, swam and played. We traveled to different areas of the country with our girls experiencing life and the world.

As time went by, our careers and social life were consuming more of our time and energy. As more responsibilities snuck into our lives, our priorities were being adjusted. We thought we could juggle it all.

My children touched the core of my soul. All the love I felt was freely expressed with them. As they grew, our deepest feelings were shared. We laughed and cried and yelled together and it was all okay. The piece of me hidden behind the veil for so long was revealed in the intimate moments of being a mother.

But engaged in the world, I resumed my position of doing. Little attention was given to feelings in our marriage. I had buried the feeling me deep in my suitcases of life and Tim was busy in activities, which defined him. Expressing feelings was not something he grew up learning either. When a conflict arose, we each resorted to behaviors we learned as small children. I lashed out in verbal attacks and he built a wall of silence around him; both burying the feelings we couldn't adequately communicate. It is a challenge to nurture relationships and live in the busyness of the world. But our mutual love for our children and each other glued us together to continue to learn the art of communication and relationships.

A sense of restlessness resided within me. All the activities of our life were fulfilling and yet a void inside kept showing its face. The love I felt for my children was the connection to my heart I had disconnected from so long ago. The yearning for another child to share that love burned inside me again. And nine months later, we welcomed

Connor Bob into our lives. He was the most amazing little bundle of joy filled with contentment and peace. Holding him I felt the connection to God and the abundant love available to us.

I cried at the thought of leaving him behind as I left for my job. My work became a burden with little nourishment for my heart. I wanted something more in my life's work; something with meaning that would benefit others in the world. How would I find that in this crazy world? My heart was opening and I began to feel more restlessness. Messages crept in. I felt a nudge to help others through difficult times, but didn't know where to turn.

Consumed once again with the activities of three small children and my career, each day I put one foot in front of the other to survive the day. I began to realize I was missing out on some valuable moments with my children and wanted to spend more time with them. I reduced my work to four days a week which was a tremendous relief knowing I had one more day to spend with these amazing kids.

What a gift the love of children brought to my life. I began to feel again. The veil I had so carefully constructed around my heart was beginning to thin. I became more connected to how I was feeling and quickly saw how my life was controlling me. I was caught in the wheel of life, spinning so fast I didn't know how to jump off. The fear of the unknown consumed me.

Who am I any way? What am I doing with my life I was given? Am I truly happy?

All these questions swirled within me for months. Physically I was exhausted. I didn't know how I could do one more thing. Mentally I began to feel out of control. Unfortunately, Tim was unavailable to help due to his added responsibility of managing the construction of a new county fairground. His career was going very well and with that came responsibilities within the community on a variety of councils and boards.

Unsure of where to turn, I took a leave of absence for a few days and the kids and I went camping in northern Minnesota. Enjoying the peace of the outdoors and the companionship of my sister and my children, I realized something had to change in my life. Looking outside of myself again, I constructed a plan to rearrange my activities and responsibilities. Upon returning from our adventure in the woods, I scheduled an appointment with a psychologist. I needed to talk to someone.

Since this was a new experience for me, I was apprehensive and somewhat nervous on my first visit. The psychologist introduced herself and asked why I had come. I began with an extensive and elaborate story of my life. I explained that I was struggling with managing my life and needed her help to plan, schedule and accomplish all the activities on my list. She boldly laughed and then realized I was serious. Then she emphatically stated, "No one can do or should do what you have just laid out in front of me. If you continue to do what you are doing something in your life will have to give. You will lose you job, something will happen with your kids, you will lose your husband or you will lose your health, to name just a few!" I was shocked! I was sure it was possible to be superwoman! Weren't other woman doing it?

I walked away that day feeling beat up and defeated. All I had known since I was a small child was success depends on all the things you do. Acceptance and love were dependent on your success. Now a new messenger walked into my life and opened my heart a little more. Something deep within was nudged awake.

One memorable night overwhelmed with life, I laid in bed with tears streaming down my face praying for change. "I don't know how to get off this spinning wheel, please help me! Whatever it takes, I am ready."

Three months later on a snowy afternoon, the call came in that would change my life forever.

Chapter 5

Is There Another Way?

"Heal the Whole: Body, Mind and Spirit." The message I heard was so profound! Where had it come from? Where can I get more?

Now looking death in the face, I chose to live. I chose to live for my children first and to teach them all about life. My heart ached for the pain and loss they were experiencing. I wanted a life of peace and happiness for them without the pain of losing a mother. Examining my life, I now saw the part of me I had buried. I felt so deeply the loving and gentle spirit that was really me. The veil was thinning again and the knowingness from within peeked its head out. I was finally able to hear.

I remembered what Dr. James told me about visualization after my surgery and began researching alternative forms of healing. I searched for naturopathic doctors, books and any other resources that could help me heal my whole self. I found a book called *A Cancer Battleplan*, written by Anne Frahm. She had cancer and survived. I was determined to do what she did.

All of this information on alternative or natural healing was completely new to me. I spoke with my doctors about it, but it was clearly news to them, too. I had to continue this battle on my own.

In the spring of 1996, I began an eleven day juice fast to cleanse my body of toxins that had built up for the past thirty-six years. During those eleven days, I lived on carrot juice, apple juice and water. I administered coffee enemas twice a day and cleansed my liver and gall bladder with olive oil and lemon juice. Looking back, it's amazing to me what one will do in desperation.

I learned the appropriate foods to eat and the liquids to drink. I studied vitamins, minerals, greens, enzymes and a variety of nutritional supports. At the end of the fast, I slowly began to eat again.

I can't even recall everything I drank and ate, but I ate a vegetarian diet and organic foods. I used a variety of vitamins, minerals, tinctures and mixtures, even shark cartilage. I was careful to drink purified water and learned to drink tea. I drank Essiac tea, Pau D'arco tea and green tea. These were all known to help cancer patients. I continued to read and learn and read and learn.

My friends and family thought I was crazy. They didn't say much, but when they did they questioned my approach. They were all skeptics. This was incredibly difficult, because I believed I needed their support and encouragement to continue to heal.

Slowly I began to understand that the reason I'd never heard much about alternative healing was that neither the medical community nor the general public accepted it. Nobody really wanted to know what I was doing for my treatment. People avoided me so they wouldn't have to ask how I was feeling or discuss cancer with me. Even Tim retreated into himself. In other people's eyes, resorting to alternative methods must have seemed like giving up, but I was nowhere near giving up.

In April of 1996, I found my first naturopathic doctor. Since this was so new to us, Tim and I were both skeptical at first. This doctor worked with me to balance the biochemical processes of my body. I did urine and saliva testing and hair analysis which told him where to begin treatment.

After the trauma of all the surgeries and treatments, my body's systems and organs continued to show symptoms of stress. Along with the continual flu-like symptoms I experienced, my thyroid gland had quit functioning. My metabolism changed, my energy level fell and I was a mess. I had hope (if not yet faith) in natural healing, and I worked with the naturopath to heal one organ and system at a time.

I was now seeing my oncologist every two months. At each visit, I had a CAT scan to check for new tumor growth. Because the earlier tumor had grown so fast, my doctors were extremely concerned about the cancer spreading to other organs. Every time I saw my oncologist, she gave me a breast exam. After a while I was so uncomfortable with it, I couldn't even ask why. She never checked the original tumor site on my leg or performed a thorough skin check. It was as if she had forgotten I had melanoma.

Tim was exhausted from it all and decided he didn't want to accompany me to appointments and tests any more. He was busy with work and the kids and needed a break. He needed some normalcy in his life again. I, on the other hand, couldn't imagine ever having a normal life again.

Summer came and went that year as it had the year before. I missed sharing it with my kids. I couldn't participate in most of their activities because of the fatigue, but they were very patient and content. It was hard for them to see their mom spend most of her days in bed, but they are strong kids with huge hearts.

I worried that other people thought I should "just get with it." I would later realize that I was the one who thought I should just be able to get up and be okay. Otherwise, it wouldn't have mattered what anyone thought. I had begun using visualization techniques after my first diagnosis of melanoma. I would visualize the cancer cells and then a healthy body destroying them. It was the first time in my life I had ever gotten still enough to listen to my body. In that process I had learned that we could do miraculous things with our minds and spirits. Now, I learned to meditate.

Meditation was quite an experience. My whole life prior to cancer was spent running around like a crazy woman. Now I had to be still enough to get quiet both inside and out, with no thoughts buzzing in my head. This was a challenge at first, but with a lot of practice I began to have tremendous control over my thoughts, as well as my breathing and my energy field.

Somewhere along the way I learned about Pathways, a health crisis resource center for people with life-threatening illnesses. Practitioners volunteered their time and provided services free of charge. They performed spiritual healing, energy healing, shiatsu, different massage techniques, breathing classes, acupressure, Reiki, and kinesiology.

When I first went to Pathways, I knew something was different about the environment. It was comforting. I met and talked to people who were living a life just like mine. I obtained books and tapes from their library that began to open my mind to a world I didn't even know existed.

Some of my first sessions were pretty hilarious. The providers working with me had never met me, yet after thirty minutes they began telling me about myself. It was amazing! One of the first things I heard was, "You must start using the wisdom of your body from the neck down and forget about your head." At that time, I didn't understand the language they spoke; yet what they said resonated deep in my being.

A few providers asked what happened to me at age three, because that was an age they recognized as traumatic to me. I remained open for the experience but was puzzled by what they said. I gradually came to understand that they learned about me through my energetic body.

These wise and loving people said over and over that if I listened to my body, it would tell me the next step I should take along my life's path. Every time I walked into Pathways, I came back out feeling exhilarated. I didn't know what they were doing, but I liked it.

When I got home, though, it was back to the "regular" world. I had no one to share my experiences with. No one in my world understood this language, and I was just learning to speak it myself. The people I knew had never heard of this stuff. I'm sure they thought it was voodoo or something. All I knew was that it made me feel better. It gave me hope and a sense of peace I could live with.

So I tried hard to practice the "prescription" I'd gotten at Pathways. I worked on listening to my body, and I meditated every day. As I learned more about meditation and energy healing, I came to know I could heal my body by learning and practicing the techniques available to me.

One of the most important healing tools was – and still is – deceptively simple. I had to learn to stay in the moment. We only have this moment, right now. The past is gone, and the future may never come. This was revolutionary to me. I had lived my entire life planning the future while dredging up the past. To be present in my body, in my life, was like exploring uncharted territory.

I took yoga classes to stay strong and learned how to move my energy field. With training and practice I found I could shift energy to provide strength and vitality to the areas of my body that needed it for healing. The various healers I saw helped me identify the places where my energy was blocked and unblock it.

Healing the whole person is not a "quick fix." It takes time to retrain our body, mind, and spirit. I had spent a lifetime living disconnected to who I really was. It wasn't until my body fell apart that I was able to see that. In the process of healing, I began to notice when my spirit was singing to me. For the first time in my adult life, I was listening.

These were important changes, but they were happening first on the inside. At first, there was not any noticeable improvement in my physical limitations. My family wondered why I wasn't feeling better right away; or rather, they wondered about my faith in alternative healing since I didn't get better right away. After all, I was taking all these supplements, eating right and going to healing classes. I, too, waited and hoped each day that I would have more energy and be able to participate in the world again. But seasons came and went, and I was still on the couch or in bed most of the time.

My family wanted me back. They wanted our old life back, but I knew that cancer had changed me permanently. I believed with all my soul that I would recover physically. I also knew that I had to be different mentally and spiritually if I truly wanted that to happen.

I was excited about the new life I was discovering. But in their own ways, the members of my family grieved the loss of the life they knew. Claire struggled daily with going to school. She cried and didn't want to leave, because she was

so afraid I wouldn't be there when she came home. Fortunately, Claire's school counselor and teachers were prepared each day to comfort and support her. They allowed her to talk, write and draw to express her feelings. By doing so, they gave her tremendous tools she will be able to use throughout her life. Connor was so attached to me that we knew he had the same fears.

Carlie tried to block out the disease by filling her world with friends. She resisted it when I talked about what was going on, but then I would get a call from her at school, wanting to know if my test results had come back yet. This scary disease was with her daily, no matter how she tried to ignore it.

Each one of my kids dealt with their fear and pain in different ways. The challenge for me was to know what they needed. I didn't want this experience to haunt them for the rest of their lives. I didn't want them to become fearful, negative and withdrawn.

I decided I needed to share with them the hope I had found. I began to voice how fortunate we are when we learn lessons early in life. I pointed out how the pain had made us all stronger, more understanding and more compassionate toward others. I assured my kids that not only would we be okay, we would be better than okay. We would be able to use these gifts of understanding and compassion to help others for the rest of our lives.

Chapter 6

Life After Cancer

Months passed. In fact, several years went by, and I was still in pain. Some days I couldn't actually believe it. It was a struggle for me to make dinner or drive my kids to swimming or skating. The most menial tasks were monumental for me. I tried so hard each day and was devastated that I couldn't function in life. Some days I didn't do very well and began feeling I wasn't a good mother or a good wife. I couldn't even take care of myself.

I would try to help the kids with homework, but the pain made it so hard just to be present with them. Starting dinner was overwhelming. The normal daily activity, laughter, or squabbles would be overwhelming for me and I would fall apart. I tried so hard to be there for them, but many days I would just cry and go to my room. My kids grew up knowing I was struggling and sick anytime I went into my room and closed the door.

The most difficult part of the experience was that I felt so disconnected from other people. The world kept moving, and it seemed other people's lives moved even faster. I spent most of my days alone. Once the initial shock of my having cancer wore off, friends and relatives went back to their old lives. Gone were the extra visits and offers of help.

My husband's theory was that I had pushed everybody away with my newfound spiritual beliefs. And I may have sounded like a new convert sometimes, but I couldn't afford to pretend. I was trying to save my life. I could no longer afford to be someone I was not just to fit.

I felt neglected. It wasn't that I wanted sympathy. I wanted loving compassionate people who could show they cared about our family. They did love us, I know, but it was as if they thought ignoring it would make it go away. I was reminded of my old survival skills, the old belief that if you just keep busy doing lots of things, you'll be okay. I understand these people, because I used to believe as they did.

When I was no longer insanely busy, I didn't have anything to talk about in social situations, at least, not with the people I used to socialize with. I was back to the old pain of not fitting in. Healing that core wound was essential to my recovery from cancer. I had to find a way to forgive and move forward.

I don't mean to suggest I'm all finished with forgiving. That's a continual process. Just when I think I've let it go, something happens to let me know that the healing continues.

But I practice and continue to create new habits of being. Staying present in the moment frees me from the past baggage once carried. The continual thoughts in my head about the past are insane. The past doesn't even exist. I send love mentally to the people I need to forgive. Trying to fit in where I don't belong anymore doesn't work. And I am remembering to be respectful of others on their own journey. I find that the more I grow, the more people come into my life that I can connect to at a heart level. I'm able to go into new situations, be myself and feel safe from judgment. By letting go of the past pain, life will provide others that can understand and support me to enter my world.

I continued to see my oncologist every two months. After a year with no sign of tumor, I was allowed to increase the interval to every four months.

As part of my proactive approach to my healthcare, I received copies of all medical reports. It helped me stay current and know which questions I needed to ask. After one of my scans, I read the pathology report and noticed something new. It said I had a spot on my gall bladder that hadn't been reported before.

When I asked Dr. Barb about it, she said she wasn't sure what that was about and was going to follow up with the radiologist. Before I knew it, her office had scheduled me for surgery to remove my gall bladder. When I tried to get some answers from the doctors, they were very hesitant. I felt I was not getting the whole story, so I got a second opinion. The second opinion was that there had been no spot: there had been an error in reading the films.

I called my oncologist again to discuss these results, to see if she thought the second opinion could be right, but she wouldn't speak to me. I told the nurse I just needed to know if there had been some kind of mistake. The doctor wouldn't get on the phone or answer my question. She preferred to remove one of my organs rather than admit a mistake.

On the other hand, I continued to develop my friendship with Dr. Kay. She was my cheerleader. Although I appreciated it, I had often wondered why my case was so important to her. One day I visited her lab and viewed some melanoma slides. I was able to see malignant cells and their movement. Generally, melanoma cells are found in the epidermis and then begin moving downward into the dermis. Dr. Kay allowed me to view my tumor. My malignant cells had been in the dermis and couldn't be seen in the epidermis.

Now the picture was coming together. My first biopsy was removed on June 1, 1995 and sent to Dr. Kay's lab. She had read the biopsy, which looked normal. Six months later, Dr. Kay removed the new growth and found melanoma.

Dr. Kay felt personally responsible for the results of the first biopsy. She couldn't see the melanoma at that time. My tumor was extremely rare and most likely not a primary tumor. I think perhaps my body had already eliminated my primary tumor, but the tumor had already released cells into my blood and spread to my leg and ovary. We will never know.

Dr. Kay was humbled by this experience. When she teaches medical students, she uses my tumor cells as an example. Her message is that melanoma is unpredictable and will do anything it wants. But the impressive thing to me is how a professional person like her can remain so teachable. I don't ask that the people in my life never make a mistake; but I do ask that they have the willingness to learn from them as I continue to learn from mine.

By 1999, no one could believe the way I was fighting off the dreadful cancer cells. At every visit with my doctors, they told me they were amazed and pleasantly surprised to see me getting stronger and stronger. A local surgeon who'd been familiar with my original diagnosis once asked, "Why are you still alive?"

Another day, Dr. Penny sat down with tears in her eyes and told me how wonderful I looked. She told me how proud she was of all the things I had done to stay strong and save my life. She said two years ago she would have never guessed we would be at this moment. We discussed natural medicine and all the valuable information, techniques and products available to heal our bodies, minds, and spirits. My faith and strength led me down a path and would sustain me on this journey.

These moments helped me keep going in the midst of the disapproval I faced from friends and family. Still, healing from cancer didn't mean an end to life's challenges. Instead, it meant that I was alive for more challenges! Earlier, I had seen a brain specialist about a spot on my brain. He explained I had an arteriovenous malformation, which means I had no capillary between an artery and vein. There was some risk of bleeding, but it was unrelated to melanoma.

We chose to ignore it then, because everyone thought that melanoma would kill me before an arteriovenous malformation would. However, as time went on and I did so well, my doctors suggested I address it.

Addressing it meant stereotactic radiosurgery, during which the surgeon radiates the trouble spot in the brain. To find the area that needs to be treated, the doctor places a ring on the patient's head, fastened with pins in the forehead and back of the head. A CAT scan pictures the area to be treated, and then an angiogram further pinpoints the treatment area. My doctor explained the procedure as if it were quite routine.

I, on the other hand, found the procedure very memorable. They began by marking the location for a ring to be fitted onto my forehead. After numbing the area only slightly, they casually started screwing this thing into my head. I could feel it, and it hurt! I couldn't believe what they were doing.

Next they took me to the scan area. University doctors always travel with an entourage. As all seven of this particular entourage watched, they used tools to attach my head ring onto a metal piece of the scan table.

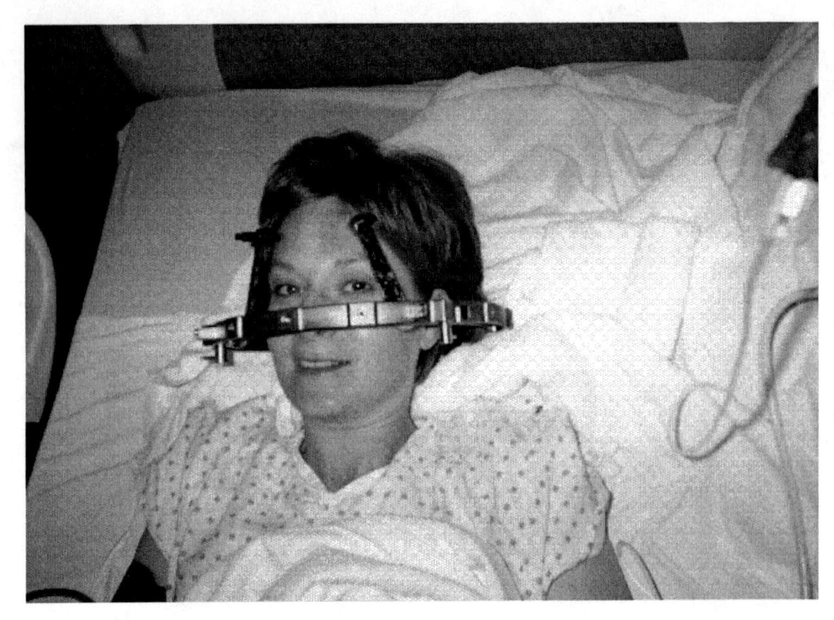

I am extremely claustrophobic, and my head was immobile. I was locked in and started to panic. I looked at Tim desperately. They all started to exit the room, and I screamed, "Where are you going, you can't leave me here alone! Have any of you ever experienced this inhumane treatment?"

"Of course not" was their reply.

Through tears I cried, "Maybe you should, so you could understand this utter helplessness."

But this group was not interested in developing empathy. They left me in the room alone. I feared I was going to hyperventilate, but I prayed for peace and strength to get through this.

I made it through the procedure and now I was not only scared and lonely, but I was angry. Thinking about how my doctor laughed when I asked for a relaxant, I said, "What gives anyone the right to treat another human with such little compassion."

Now it was time to wheel me into the next room, and I was almost in shock. A surgeon kindly greeted me. I said, "You're not going to screw me on the table like the last guy did, are you?" He did his best not to laugh, and I didn't realize until later what I had said. I bet that question will go down in medical history. I expressed how upset I was, and this surgeon kindly gave me a sedative for the angiogram.

For the angiogram, the doctors placed a tube in the artery of my right groin, strung it up to the artery in my neck and head, and then shot dye into the artery. The only hard part for me was the pressure required on the artery to stop the bleeding. That doctor placed all of his weight on my groin for thirty minutes. I was black and blue for weeks.

Next, I was off to radiation. They fastened me onto the table again to keep me immobile, but this time, thanks to the sedative, I was more relaxed. After radiation, they removed the head ring. I thought my head would explode. I had the worst headache imaginable, and all I could do for it was cry.

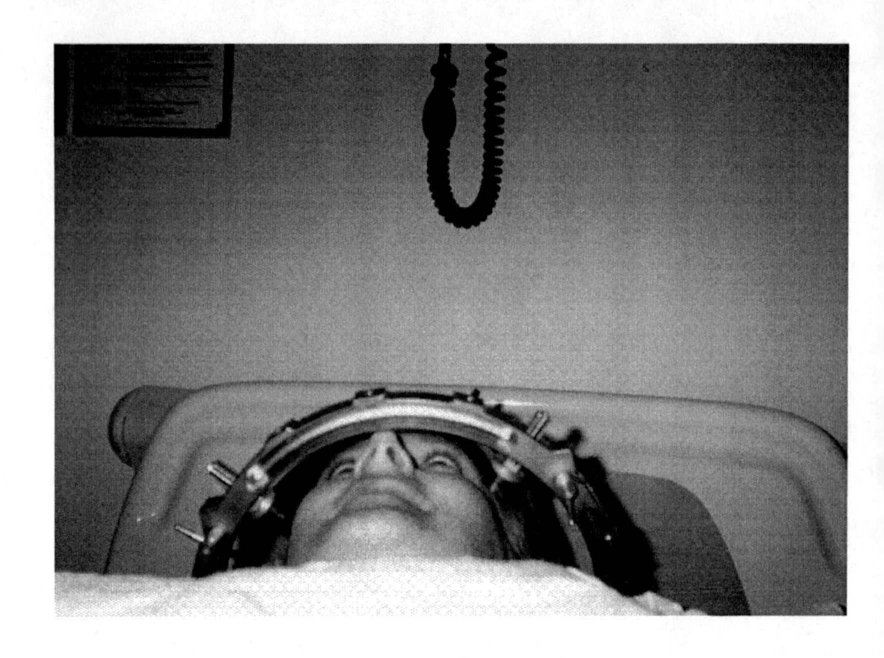

I spent the night in the hospital to make sure the catheterization of the artery caused no problems. Then the doctor casually told me I would be taking anti-seizure medication from now on. "You have got to be kidding!" I said. "You never even mentioned medication before. I won't take any meds!" He wouldn't release me from the hospital and angrily continued to bully me until I conformed.

A week later, when I had bruises covering my left leg, the doctor said they were definitely not caused from the meds, but if I would feel better he would approve a different anti-seizure medication. A few days later I was curled up in bed with severe stomach cramps. I said to Tim, "Obviously, my body is telling me something." I went off the drugs that day and never had a seizure.

Life went on and the fourth year went by with no melanoma scares, but I was still feeling terribly sick most days. My body hurt from top to bottom. The muscle aches and fatigue were overwhelming. The simplest tasks were monumental.

My inability to perform normal activities filled my heart with sadness. My inability to be present cost my husband and children so much. I continued to meditate to find a peaceful space where I could leave the pain behind. I didn't know how to live in that meditative space each and every moment, but I was sure there was a way. I dedicated myself to finding it. What was this peaceful place? Was it in me? Was it God? I didn't know. But I knew that other people had learned to live in a state of peace, and I could, too.

I read and studied the Bible daily. It raised issues and questions for me, which I discussed with others who were on a similar path. Sometimes I found spiritual and health discussion groups online, because I didn't have many people nearby to talk to about these things. My friends and family didn't want to talk about religion or spirituality, but I was on a mission. I was learning so much each day and wanted to share my discoveries.

What I didn't realize at the time was that my attempts to integrate and explain all I was learning frightened some people away from me. It was bitterly ironic: Here I was, a person who had wanted nothing more than to fit in my whole life, and now all I could do was keep people at a distance. The things I was learning seemed strange and threatening to them, and I was so intrigued with it all that I didn't always see how it affected them. That was true of many friends and family, even my husband.

Tim and I coped the best we could, but as time passed I began to feel distance growing between us. I could see Tim going through the motions, trying to be two parents, with little or no emotion. Many nights I tried to give him an opportunity to voice how he was feeling, but he was so busy trying to survive he couldn't afford to go into his feelings. He could only talk about schedules and kids. Tim was afraid I would die, and he was trying to prepare himself for that by keeping a wall between us.

The wall helped Tim to survive my illness in the short run, but he grew just as lonely inside of the wall as I was outside of it. I wanted to draw closer and be comforted, but his grief over the life we had lost to cancer had hardened into anger. Even though he knew I couldn't turn back the clock, he couldn't help but be angry at me for getting sick and ending our old lives. Yet he couldn't express that to me back then. He didn't know how to allow himself to be angry with a sick person. Sadly, because Tim was trying so hard to be the "good" husband, taking care of everything without complaining, our marriage became dishonest. I sensed he was angry, but if I addressed feelings at all, the wall went up.

Although I couldn't provide much day-to-day care, I continued to communicate with the kids and be open to their concerns and fears. We kept life as normal as possible, but the pain in their young eyes came through. They could feel the fear and tension in our home. I feared this would create beliefs about themselves that would affect them forever. Tim provided the physical care that I couldn't, and I tried to provide the emotional care that he couldn't. It wasn't perfect – in fact, it was very painful a lot of the time – but we both did the best we could do.

Tim Ice Fishing with Claire and Connor

The kids had many questions about life and death. They had already experienced the death of their great-grandma and grandfather, so they were comfortable asking questions. I saw an opportunity for them to understand life while they were exploring the potential death of their mother. They wanted to know about heaven and what it was like. They actively discussed with each other the ramifications of burial versus cremation. One time, four-year-old Connor asked, "Mom, are you going to be creamed?" Another day we were driving by a cemetery when Claire exclaimed, "It would be a lot easier, Mom, if you just decided how you were going to be buried!" It continually amazed me how this illness was with my kids every day.

Life is a journey of remembering who we really are. During these talks with my children, I came to see that they had a much better understanding of who they really are than we adults do. My children came to understand that we would be together forever and that our time on Earth is just a split second compared to eternity.

Claire was especially close to her spiritual being. She knew that no matter what happened, I would be with her in spirit always. She wanted me to promise I would give her a sign, to leave a note in her room to tell her I was there. I assured her that when the time comes, she will know I am there.

As I continued to work with naturopathic doctors and homeopathic health practitioners, I began to trust that what I needed to do next would present itself at the right time. I learned to call forth the people and the tools I needed to help me continue healing. Amazingly, the right person always appeared at just the right time.

One example of this synchronicity was the day I collapsed with excruciating pain in my head. The ambulance took me to hospital, where the doctors thought my brain was hemorrhaging. So they rushed me to another hospital where I met a whole team of doctors. An Asian woman standing near my bed whispered to someone else, "It almost sounds muscular to me."

Days later, I went to see a chiropractor. He described my neck and shoulder muscles as being "shrink-wrapped" by tension. No oxygen was getting there. That's what was causing the terrible headache pain, and he was able to give me relief.

Throughout my life, I was unaware of such beautiful synchronicities. I was out of touch with who I was and what my heart and soul were telling me. I did not see the perfection. But I was learning the perfection had always been there. I had attached myself to destructive beliefs I carried with me in my suitcases my entire life.

Throughout my life, I had tried to connect with my mom. I had hoped to make her understand, love and accept me in a way that I could recognize. However, I would walk away from a "fun" day of shopping with her and feel more lonely and distant than before. I believed that she did not accept and love me for who I was, so I experienced feeling unloved every time I was with her.

As I healed from cancer, I began to see the same themes repeated over and over in my life. The beliefs I carried all these years were created by me. I began to ask myself, "What other beliefs am I carrying? Am I really creating all this pain and suffering?" It was miraculous to feel who I really was and to see the power I had to create my beliefs and life experiences.

I was peeling layers and layers of beliefs away to see the real me. In my heart, I knew who I was. I could feel it. But then my experiences would contradict this knowingness from within. What was God trying to tell me? Could I really be creating my pain and illness? Could I really be creating my life by my thoughts and beliefs?

Passing through a bookstore, I picked up a book called *Ask and It Is Given*, by Jerry and Esther Hicks. I wasn't familiar with the authors, but I was drawn to the book, so I bought it. A couple of days later, I felt I should start a discussion group on the book, which I hadn't even read yet. Then I read an online article I like a lot, and I saw that the author of the article lived not far from me. I sent an email, and we set a date to meet and have coffee.

In the meantime, I attended a marketing meeting and met several new people. The day I met the writer for coffee, she mentioned that some of her friends had talked about meeting me at a gathering. I was shocked that all these new people were connected to each other, and even more shocked to realize I was already linked to them in some way. I said, "I have this new book and was considering a book group to discuss it."

She replied, "Oh my God, I have been studying Jerry and Esther Hicks for years and have been looking for a group!"

More synchronicities, but they were no longer coincidences. Instead, they were like instruments of a symphony, coming in and playing their part at exactly the right time. Not long ago I was unable to hear the song of my soul. But now, I could hear the song. Even more amazing to me, who'd grown up feeling so alone, I saw people dance in and out of my life with perfect timing, as if they could hear the song, too.

Chapter 7

Awakening

In my deepest pit of darkness and pain, I cried out to anyone who would hear. My heart was breaking from loneliness. I didn't know how to pull myself out of the depths of darkness, so I called out to God to show me the way. Out of my heart came the song of my soul. Time stood still as my hand wrote the words of pain that streamed out of my entire being. I was opening the door and uncovering the veil to my soul.

Pain and suffering and tears consumed me far too long. I had lived my entire life with beliefs that had created tremendous suffering. Now ten additional years had past, and this ugly disease had eaten away the most valuable years of my life. The sadness I felt enveloped me. Was it really the disease causing this pain and suffering? Did I walk this path of hell for a purpose? So many questions flooded in. Did I choose this path, but why? After the darkest days, I have always believed a brilliant rainbow would miraculously appear. Where is the rainbow?

The veil thinned and for brief moments was completely lifted. I woke up and saw so clearly who I was and how I created my life. I forgot who I was born to be. As a young child, I was connected to my spirit, but I largely lost that connection by adjusting to the physical world. I slowly lost that spirit within and forgot how to listen to the still small voice of my soul. Many times throughout my life, I heard, but didn't listen. I was distracted. Through the years, little by little, I lost the connection to my spirit. I became my body and mind and the activities they could perform. Then I walked through time believing these activities defined who I was, and I became the activities.

I had spent my lifetime running in circles doing all the things I thought I was suppose to do. I wanted to be accepted by the world. I searched endlessly outside of myself for that acceptance and love. Sure, I had fun and exciting life experiences in college, while traveling, raising my children and in my career. But I was moving through time disconnected from the pure joy that comes from God and from within. The distractions of life allowed me to keep the door to my soul closed. I felt empty at times, as if a piece of me was missing. Life didn't flow naturally and easily. I was pushing against something which I couldn't identify. I was pushing against me. I didn't stop to recognize the signs of dis-ease. I was caught in the spinning wheel of life thinking I was unable to get off. Until that fateful night, calling out to God, "Please help me, whatever it takes, I am ready." Diagnosed with stage 4 malignant melanoma was my wake up call.

I had chosen to stay imprisoned by my thoughts and beliefs I adopted as a very young child. Were these beliefs still a part of me? Did I still believe I was unacceptable?. Did I believe I had to continue to prove my worth? Did I believe I had to earn love? These beliefs I had carried in my suitcases far too long and created many painful experiences in my life. I didn't want to experience that pain any more.

My process of healing was a journey to find myself again. That free spirited, loving child within was reborn. In order to experience life, I had to experience death, death of my old self.

With this knowingness, information and books about others who had walked this path of awakening appeared. I soon discovered we all have adopted beliefs as children that create the experiences we have in this lifetime. I examined the beliefs I carried and laughed out loud, “Is this really the answer? Could it really be this simple?” All the prophets and wise ones I studied and frantically searched for the answer were all saying the same thing. “Is this what they were telling me all along?” A sense of peace and truth filled me as if I had always known. Within I have always been me, connected to God and the infinite universe with unlimited potential to do and be anything I chose.

In those moments of complete peace and awareness, I saw that I am love. I didn’t have to search outside of myself for acceptance and love.

That peaceful place I had found years earlier was my connection to God and my true self. Many have come before us calling this place by many names, God, Buddha, higher self, universe, Jesus, Krishna and more. The process used is called many things on earth; prayer, meditation, stillness, connection, alone in nature. The word chosen to describe the profound love and awareness doesn’t matter. The journey is about creating and experiencing so we can remember who we are and live in joy.

When I allowed the flow of love from God to move through me in the moment of now, true joy and happiness was found. The peace found in those brief moments of clarity is profound. The yearning for more consumes the conscious mind. All the beliefs and thoughts of yesterday are truly gone in this very moment. My mind can let go and be completely present in the moment. This is God and our inheritance. This is what I came to experience.

I want my children always to remember how powerful they are and know they are truly children of God. They were created in His image. Their inheritance is abundance in all areas of their life, especially love and joy. When listening to their thoughts about school, friends, sports and life, I help them see how their thoughts are creating what they are or will be experiencing.

Sometimes children learn the lessons even better than we do. My son Connor believed that he was a good hockey player even when his skills were average. He decided he wanted to be a part of the top hockey team his first year. He wrote that down and said it out loud.

Tim and I didn't want to discourage him, but to be honest we were concerned that Connor would get hurt. We knew he worked hard, but we also knew his skills didn't seem advanced enough for that level of play. When his coach called with the results of the tryouts, he welcomed Connor to the "A" team. I was shocked, but Connor said, "Mom, I knew I'd make the "A' team!" He never wavered in his belief, and he created the reality he wanted.

Our reality is created by our thoughts and feelings. Everything we see in our outer world is a direct reflection of our inner world. What we focus on most is exactly what is showing up in our life. Focusing our attention on problems in life, what we don't have, and all the bad things will only give us more of what we don't want. So if we want great health and abundance, peace and happiness in our lives and the world, let's give our attention to that.

Most of the time, I was unconscious of what my focus was. During my healing years, I lived with so much pain and fatigue; I was unaware of my attention on the pain and misery. When I was praying or meditating, I could eliminate the pain. I was no longer focusing on my physical being and was connected to God and my spirit. It took me years to really understand and experience something different.

I am here to tell you, STOP! You do not have to live life suffering. Knowing I could choose something different, I realized I could discard my old suitcases forever and live the life I choose.

Now in difficult or uncomfortable situations, I stop and check in with myself to see what I am thinking and feeling. I stand outside of myself and watch the incessant thoughts. I become the observer. Many times these thoughts existed in the past, and I would create more suffering if I didn't stop and let them go. In that moment, I can choose. I am continually amazed by how powerful our creation process is. We live in a world that is consumed with negative thinking habits. It is impossible to monitor all of our thoughts and words. Because we have millions of thoughts a day, we were born with emotions to use as our guide. We cannot possibly control all our thoughts. I pay attention to how something feels. If something doesn't feel good, it is message to take notice. What is it I need to look at and deal with? What should I remember here? Is this who I really am or what I really want?

Old habits of behavior and thinking continue through my process of awakening. We all have habits of thoughts and beliefs that can be broken. To know something in your heart and soul is profound. To know something in your mind is reassuring. But to experience what you know in your mind and feel it in your heart is enlightening.

When I am struggling, I am paddling against my natural current of life and I remind myself to turn around and flow with the current. All good things happen when I am connected to the natural stream of well-being. When I am present and hear that voice of God from within, well-being flows, answers to questions come and a profound truth is revealed.

I have walked this path to feel and experience the awakening of my soul. I lived in the suffering I created and know the hopelessness of the human condition. I felt the isolation and loneliness. I know what it feels like to want to end the suffering, as if you can't take another step in this world. I know the feeling of rejection and abandonment in the world. I know the feeling of physical pain and exhaustion. I know the unbearable emotional pain. I had to live it, to know it in the deepest part of my soul.

And the rainbow always appears! Through the deepest, darkest valley, I found the light! That slight whisper singing within was heard. The pure joy and love of who we are is screaming to be heard in each of us. Our paths are different, but we are all on the same journey home. Throughout our lifetimes, we have messengers along the way to help us find our way. May I be one of those messengers for you.

Little did I know where this journey would end. I guess I still don't, and it doesn't matter. I am learning to enjoy the adventure. Resting in the knowingness that the perfect experience will happen today or NOW.

Another year and I am grateful for the miracles we have experienced in our lives. I am grateful to be alive and watch and experience my children growing and living life. When this journey began, I could have never imagined this year and all we have experienced through this whole cancer journey.

Connor Carlie Claire

This year began with a knowingness from within to start cleansing my physical body. I followed my heart and had no idea where this journey would take me. I only felt a need to clean out the old and begin putting clean, healthy nutrients back in a clean body. Just another step to be taken on my journey. I am learning to trust.

When we remove the old (no matter what it is) there is room available for the new. This is true in cleaning out old clothes, or dealing with a painful experience, or facing a negative relationship, or any experience in life. The cleansing began to prepare the way for removing the old and making room for something new. When we listen and trust God leads us and guides us on our journey. I was ready to listen and trust that my next step would be provided. I was cleaning my intestines and colon and eating good organic food, when the opportunity landed at my door to go to Tulum.

My body was prepared for the experiences in Tulum. I was able to physically endure the exercises including yoga, pilates and cardio. I was mentally clearer to be present. Being present in conversations with the other women, with yoga, or my healing sessions or in the sweat lodge all allowed me to truly be there and experience it. I was clearer as emotions came up and I was able to feel, see and experience them. Then I could let them go forever.

A calm and peace appears as we are present and connected to God and our true self. This awareness is comforting and peaceful. We are able to see and know things we didn't before. Answers to questions appear, and guidance on decisions is available.

So this was an amazing plan. Not a plan I was consciously aware of, but a plan that I trusted and followed. Tulum was a healing and growth process. I feel as if I shedded another layer or layers of "stuff" I have been carrying around this human body. As I shed more "stuff", new "stuff" arrives. I anxiously wait for more new stuff. What do I mean by stuff?

Well, new exciting experiences are coming my way, new rewarding relationships, new opportunities to do what I love, new opportunities to help other people, new information I never heard about........the list goes on and on. This is life! So let's enjoy the adventure together!

My Family Today - Claire, Sheila, Connor, Carlie, Tim

Today I continue my healing journey, adding to all I have experienced, for the journey of remembering who I really am. I create my life each day, and all good things are available to me. I am energy in a universe of energy. I am love. We are created in the image of God, to experience the greatness we are. Love heals all things and peace, happiness, abundance and joy are our inheritance.

My journey to wellness is truly an awakening to the Song of My Soul!

"I share my story of healing with you so all of us will heal and find our magnificent selves. Through speaking and coaching, I am helping others find hope and live with passion and joy. Together as we live our greatness, we will create a loving, peaceful world. Join us in lifting up humanity to live in love and joy!"

Get your free report, "Survive Cancer",
at www.sheilaulrich.com

Truly Alive
Sheila Ulrich
www.sheilaulrich.com
sheila@sheilaulrich.com
320.282.9722